# A SPECIAL EDITION FOR RESIDENTS AND FRIENDS of SAUSALITO

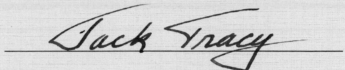

JACK TRACY·SAUSALITO, CALIFORNIA
DECEMBER, NINETEEN EIGHTY THREE

———————————◆———————————

Number: _75_

# SAUSALITO

*Moments in Time*

## *Acknowledgements*

It is impossible to list all the people who have contributed directly or indirectly to this effort. With all due respect, *Sausalito, Moments in Time* is for them. The resources of the Sausalito Historical Society, National Maritime Museum, Bancroft Library, and California Historical Society were invaluable.

For some time this book has been whirling about in my mind. Thank you Wayne and Linda Bonnett for encouraging me to put it down on paper.

J. T.

PHOTO CREDITS
All photographs are from the Sausalito Historical Society
except as otherwise identified.

Research Consultation, Elizabeth Robinson
Copy Editing, Stephen McElroy, Marian G. Witwer
Contemporary Photos, Christiansen Photography
Production Assistance, Martha Tuescher
Transcriptions, Shirley Norman
Historic Photo Prints, Noubar Demerjian, Color 2000, San Francisco
Typography, Burch & McElroy & Heisch, Mill Valley, California
Printing, Paragraphics, San Rafael, California
Camera Work, Stephen Abramson, Paragraphics
Binding, Cardoza-James, San Francisco

Published in the United States of America

Windgate Press
P.O. Box 1715, Sausalito, California, 94965

First Printing December 1983

ISBN 0-915269-00-7

*"Settle in Sausalito;*
*Live Long and Be Happy."*
Sausalito News, *first issue,*
*February 12, 1885*

*To Janet,*
*Elizabeth, Thomas, Stephen, and Alison,*
*that they will remember their moments.*

# SAUSALITO
## Moments in Time

*A Pictorial History of Sausalito's*
*First One Hundred Years:*
*1850-1950*

## by Jack Tracy

*Edited by Wayne Bonnett*

*Designed by Linda Witwer Bonnett*

*Sausalito, California, in a 1967 photograph, looking south, with San Francisco just across the Golden Gate Bridge. Fort Baker is to the left of the bridge on the Marin side. Highway 101 winds down Waldo Grade to Sausalito's northern waterfront in the lower portion of the picture, dominated by the Marinship site. The houseboat community is at the lower edge, and Marin City is at lower right. The vast open space west of Sausalito is now part of the Golden Gate National Recreation Area.*

Sausalito, Moments in Time
*is about this town.*

*Sausalito Yacht Harbor, with the "Hill" as a backdrop in this contemporary photo.*

*Early morning in Sausalito.*

*Sausalito is a place of unique and somewhat fragile charm.*

*Dunphy Park on Richardson's Bay.*

Plaza Viña del Mar.

Old City Hall Building today.

*Much of its character is a reflection of the character of the residents.*

*Public pathway on Bulkley Avenue*

*Christ Church.*

*On the Sausalito Sea Wall.*

*Interior, Casa Madrona Hotel*

*Before: Princess Street, 1910*

*After: Princess Street, 1983*

$M$any people during the course of many years have contributed wittingly or unwittingly to the development of Sausalito's character. Sausalito has been shaped not only by local events in the area of San Francisco Bay but by national and international occurrences as well. The town has lived through real-estate speculations, wild schemes, political intrigues, and wartime upheavals. It has had its share of bad press, both deserved and undeserved. Yet through it all, Sausalito has evolved as a special place that evokes a warm response in visitors from all over the world. That feeling comes from the character of Sausalito, its past and present, and from the common bond of an uncommon love of a town by its inhabitants.

As a natural outgrowth of an increasing interest in documenting and preserving Sausalito's past, the Sausalito Historical Society was formed in 1975. As its collection grew, of artifacts, photos, and other memorabilia donated by residents past and present, it became apparent that a visual record should follow.

Now, perhaps more than ever before, Sausalitans have come to regard their town as a place of unique and somewhat fragile charm. In 1980, with a great deal of public support, a Sausalito Historic District encompassing many of the original downtown buildings was created. The following year, the District was certified by the Department of Interior.

These efforts by Sausalito residents to recognize and protect some of what has evolved stem in part from an awareness of what has been lost by other communities. As Director of the Historical Society, I have often been asked about the town's history. But never has the question been more charmingly put than in this letter from a man in a small town in Utah:

> "I was through your town recently and was very impressed as to how you have developed such a beautiful and unique theme. Our city is contemplating developing a theme, and restructuring our existing buildings after that theme.
>
> Could you relate to us how the idea of that theme began in your city? Also, would you relate the struggles and things to be watchful for as the idea begins to become a reality? If you could send some 'before and after' pictures, I would be glad to reimburse you."

This book is in part, a response to that letter.
I hope it answers his questions.
Jack Tracy
December, 1983

*Bronze sea lion by Albert Sybrian.*

$E$arly on the afternoon of August 5, 1775, Lieutenant Don Juan Manuel de Ayala aboard his vessel *San Carlos* at the entrance to San Francisco Bay ordered the longboat lowered alongside. He sent his first mate and pilot Don José de Canizares, along with several crewmen, to find a safe anchorage within the huge bay that lay before them. Thus Canizares became the first European to enter the Golden Gate from the sea, and the first to view the panorama of the bay and see the coves and hills of what would become Sausalito.*

Over the next six weeks as Ayala and his crew explored this wondrous bay, Canizares recorded their finds. According to his record, the *San Carlos* anchored off Sausalito during part of their explorations. The area was abundant with timber: tall firs for ships' masts and spars and oak for planking. The hills abounded with deer, elk, and

bear; the bay with clams, shrimp, salmon, and abalone. The shores teemed with sea lions, seals, and otters. The bay was an unspoiled paradise.

Canizares documented the existence of Indian villages surrounding the bay, including one on the future site of Sausalito. The Indian inhabitants of these villages, the Coastal Miwoks (called by the Spanish *Nación de Uimen*) greeted the newcomers with friendship and curiosity. In describing the bay, Ayala reported glowingly: "To all these advantages must be added the best of all, which is that the heathen Indians of the port are so faithful in their friendship and so docile in their disposition that I was greatly pleased to receive them on board."

The *Uimen,* according to Canizares, were indeed friendly and hospitable; they appeared well fed and healthy. Their dwellings on the site of Sausalito were explored and mapped in 1907 nearly a century and a half later by an archaeological survey. By that time, nothing was left of the culture of those who had first enjoyed the natural treasures of the bay. The life of the Coastal Miwoks had been reduced to archaeological remnants, as though thousands of years had passed since their existence.

In the same year as Ayala's bay exploration, Juan Bautista de Anza was charged with the establishment of a permanent *presidio* or military garrison. De Anza had blazed a trail overland from Sonora across the desert to *Mission San Gabriel* near the pueblo of *Los Angeles,* in order to avoid the arduous sea passage north from Mexico against prevailing winds. He and his soldiers had safely brought to San Gabriel 240 colonists on this first of many planned journeys overland. From San Gabriel he marched up the coast from mission to mission until he reached the bay.

According to Spanish plans, de Anza's route would open all of upper California to colonization and provide a reliable pathway for supplies to the new colony. But the once-cooperative Yuma Indians over whose lands the trail passed attacked and destroyed the isolated trail settlements along the way. Hence, Spain was forced to fall back on the ocean route to supply her northern colonies. Failure to establish an overland passage meant that what the Spanish called *Alta California,* supplied only by sea, would remain remote and undercolonized for many years, a fact that would bear heavily on California's fate when, decades later, Americans began arriving in large numbers.

Life in the provinces of New Spain reflected few of the changes occurring in Europe. Outward change came slowly in the small pueblos and missions in California during the last two decades of the eighteenth century. Daily life there alternated between a difficult pastoral existence and an outright struggle against famine and disease. Captured or lured to the missions, the Native Americans, now universally called "Indians," became serfs on the land and forced converts into the Church. Soldiers of the Crown who had risked their lives with Portola and de Anza were rewarded with land grants, large tracts of real estate at first intended as little more than grazing rights. These later grew into a pivotal political issue for Californians.

Concerned by the growing vulnerability of her overseas colonies, Spain laid down rigid laws to protect her investments abroad. Instructions from the Crown, via Mexico City, to the governor of *Alta California,* were explicit: foreign ships and foreign visitors were not to enter Spanish territory. The less other nations saw of the miles of fertile land, fine harbors and rich forests (and the thin scattering of Spanish occupants), the better. However, the hundreds of miles of open coastline and the increasing number of fur trappers in Pacific waters made it inevitable that other Europeans would find their way into Spanish ports.

The first non-Spanish ship came in 1786 and anchored off Monterey. Le Comte de Laperouse, under orders from the French government, was stopping over briefly on his "voyage of discovery." In reality, of course, he was looking for potential French colonies, and, more specifically, to see what Spain was up to in California. In defiance of edicts from the Spanish Crown, Laperouse was welcomed; and he learned all there was to learn about Spanish defenses and commerce. Before sailing off to an unknown fate at sea, he ventured the opinion that there was little in upper California to interest France or any other European power for at least one to two hundred years.

The next non-Spanish explorer to show up on the northern coast was George Vancouver of England, who landed in San Francisco Bay in 1792. He too was welcomed and even escorted overland to Monterey for further receptions. It should be mentioned that the governor was away at the time, and when he heard of the hospitality shown the foreigner, he was, to put it mildly, not amused. Least welcome of all foreigners were the Americans. Either because these "Boston Yanquis" were considered particularly aggressive, or because their antimonarchist, Protestant republic was on the same continent as California, Americans were forbidden absolutely to land in San Francisco Bay.

In time, as a new governor took over in Monterey, American ships were permitted to lay over long enough to take on food and supplies and to off-load their sick; the first of these was the ship *Otter* in 1796. The Spanish residents even grew to like and accept some of these "Yanquis." Of necessity, the Spanish also began simple trade with foreign visitors, even though this too was illegal. In this period ships first came to the cove in Sausalito for fresh water before setting out to sea.

By 1795 the age of innocence was over for California. Word of its natural wonders had reached the courts and governments of Europe. Although, as Laperouse had predicted, it was not yet practical to pursue aggressive colonization, still it was attracting increasing interest. Then the flow of newcomers to the New World slowed to a trickle while Napoleon and his armies were overrunning Europe. But the time was clearly coming. For in 1795 there had occurred in England an event unrecorded in history then, but of primary importance to our story now: William Richardson was born.

---

* To avoid confusion, the modern spelling of *Sausalito* is used throughout this book, even during the period of history when *Saucelito* was the accepted spelling. Exceptions are when *Saucelito* appears as the name of something other than the town, such as the ferryboat *Saucelito.* See page 181 for the origins of the two spellings.

William Antonio Richardson is in many ways an elusive figure in Sausalito history. His early years and his first ventures at sea are undocumented. When he arrived in San Francisco Bay in 1822, he was twenty-seven and was first mate on the British whaler *Orion.* By that time he had been master of his own vessel and was an experienced navigator, carpenter, and shipwright. He spoke a smattering of several languages and was fluent in Spanish. His years at sea had made him a survivor, well suited for a life of adventure.

What is known of Richardson is enough to establish him as the founder of Sausalito as well as of Yerba Buena, now San Francisco. In his thirty-four years in California until he died in 1856, Richardson was not only a ship master, cartographer, and navigator, but also rancher, businessman, bureaucrat, and family man. A man of diverse aspects, he was described by his contemporaries as "a swindler and opportunist" and, conversely, as a man who "had not a single enemy" and was "kind, honest, and generally beloved."

When Richardson arrived in California, Mexico had just won her independence from Spain. San Francisco Bay colonization, like that of other remote Spanish outposts, had suffered years of neglect. There were two settlements: the mission, *San Francisco de Assís* and the military garrison, *El Presidio,* with no more than several dozen non-Indian inhabitants between them. Attempts to establish a *pueblo,* or town, had failed. There was nothing at the place called Yerba Buena but sand dunes and thickets. Captain Frederick Beechey, of *H.M.S. Blossom,* an English explorer who visited in 1826, described the Presidio as "little better than a heap of rubbish on which jackals, dogs and vultures were constantly preying."

Richardson remained behind at the Presidio when the *Orion* sailed from San Francisco Bay in 1822. His reasons for "jumping ship" are obscured by time. One romantic legend has it that he was smitten by the lovely Maria Antonia Martinez, daughter of the *Commandante* of the Presidio, Don Ignacio Martinez. Quite likely he liked what he saw in California and sensed opportunity in this "new" country. In any case he did stay, and in October, 1822, petitioned Governor Sola for permission to become a citizen of Mexico, and to become a permanent resident. His request was granted with the understanding that he would teach carpentry and navigation "to such young men as should be placed under his care." Richardson acquired several small boats and set local Indians to building more. He established a thriving business transporting grain and hides from the creeks and estuaries around the bay to the ships at anchor in Sausalito or Yerba Buena Cove. In Sausalito he supplied ships with seasoned hardwood cut by his Indians, and fresh water, always in abundant supply.

By 1825 Richardson had been baptized into the Catholic faith as required for citizenship and marriage. On May 12, 1825, he married Maria Antonia Martinez. His new father-in-law Don Ignacio, in addition to being *Comman-*

*dante* of the Presidio, was holder of a large east bay land grant. He offered a ranch to the newly-weds as a gift. But Richardson declined. He was a seaman at heart and saw cattle raising as merely a side business. He was far more intrigued by Sausalito's maritime potential.

Although Richardson lived near the Presidio during this period, his activities frequently took him to Sausalito's cove where the excellent spring water and wood supplies provided him with a steady income. Believing that one day San Francisco and Sausalito would both become important cities, he set his sights on acquiring the Marin headlands, including Sausalito with its springs. Meanwhile, John Reed, a twenty-year-old Irishman, arrived on the scene in 1826 and took an instant liking to Sausalito and the Marin hills. He made friends easily and was an energetic, popular addition to the small colony of Europeans. After building a small cabin at Sausalito's cove, he petitioned Governor Echienda for a land grant that would include Sausalito. His request was denied, but it must have startled Richardson to have another suitor wooing the Mexican governor for the very desirable tract of land. Not to be outdone, he also petitioned Echienda for the Marin headlands. Both men were no doubt aware of Mexican law that reserved islands and headlands for military purposes. Both also knew that Mexican law was sometimes strictly enforced and sometimes not.

Many years later Richardson claimed that his 1828 request for the rancho had been granted by Echienda. The formalities of title transfer were never completed, he insisted, because the papers had been lost or mislaid in Mexico City. Whatever the case, Richardson spent the next ten years attempting to gain clear title to the Sausalito grant. Mexico was obviously still reluctant to let strategically important headlands fall into private hands. In 1829 Richardson pulled up stakes, abandoned his Sausalito and San Francisco enterprises, and moved with his family to San Gabriel, then the capital of *Alta California.* The capital was alive with political intrigue as court followers maneuvered for position and plotted to gain power. There Richardson became close friends with Don José Figueroa, who had replaced Echienda as governor. In 1835, the friendship paid off when Figueroa appointed Richardson Captain of the Port of San Francisco and sent him there to establish a *pueblo,* or civilian settlement.

Once again Richardson gathered his family and belongings, and they sailed north to San Francisco. Aided by surveyors, he laid out a plan of streets and lots for the future city, and quickly applied for one lot for himself. He built the first permanent civilian residence in Yerba Buena Cove and with his wife and children became literally the first family of San Francisco. Upon his return, he had discovered to his dismay that Figueroa had granted the Marin headlands, including Sausalito, to José Antonio Galindo, a well-connected soldier at the Presidio. Nonetheless, Richardson set up shop once again in Sausalito's cove, where, as Captain of the Port, he used his abilities and connections

to full advantage. He directed incoming ships to Sausalito as usual for water and wood, but he was now charged with collecting duties and anchorage fees. It is quite likely from the sketchy evidence available that Richardson, with the aid of his father-in-law, *Commandante* of the Presidio, applied the Mexican regulations in a very uneven manner and conducted a profitable side business of imaginative recordkeeping. As a contemporary writer put it, "Richardson was full of Mexican authority and Anglo-Saxon enterprise."

José Galindo, meanwhile, was occupied with his other land grant, *Rancho Laguna de la Merced.* He had never formalized, that is, achieved *juridical possession* of under Mexican law, his Sausalito grant. Richardson pursued *his* claim to the land with the new Mexican governor and friend, Juan Bautista Alvarado, but his 1836 petition was again denied. Two years later, Galindo, who had not satisfied conditions for the grant, was accused of murdering José Peralta. A document dated 1838 does indeed name Antonio Galindo as a prisoner, but his fate is unknown. It has been suggested but never substantiated that Richardson had purchased the grant from Galindo.

In any case, on February 11, 1838, Richardson finally achieved his desire; he was given a clear title to the land, some 19,571 acres. Richardson called it *El Rancho del Sausalito;* it stretched from the Marin headlands at the Golden Gate to what is now Stinson Beach, and included the lucrative *Puerto de los Balleneros,* or Whaler's Cove, at Sausalito. John Reed, now a good friend of Richardson's had in the meanwhile become *Major Domo* of *Mission San Rafael,* married Hilaria Sanchez, daughter of a prominent Spanish family, and been granted a huge tract including present-day Mill Valley, Tiburon, Belvedere, and Corte Madera. This he called *El Rancho Corte Madera del Presidio* in recognition of his lumber business that supplied the Presidio in San Francisco.

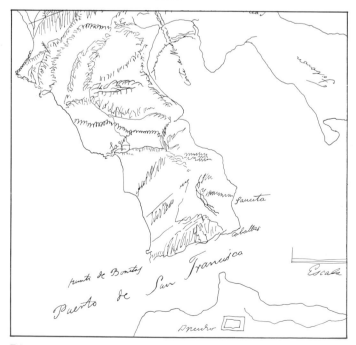

Diseño *or map accompanying Richardson's land grant application.*

It took three more years for Richardson to acquire *juridical possession* of his lands. In 1841, accompanied by his wife and children, the *Alcalde* from Sonoma, and two witnesses, Richardson traversed the boundary of his grant. They travelled on horseback, pausing at each *majonera* or landmark, where Richardson recited the required oath before witnesses. At the conclusion of the three-day journey, the *Alcalde* signed the papers stating that the petitioner had complied with "all formalities of the Law" (and there were many). Thus on October 15, 1841, the land became the undisputed property of Don Guillermo Antonio Richardson, to "enjoy freely and exclusively, appropriating it to the culture and use that best may suit him."

Richardson had ridden over almost every acre of the ranch and walked the long shoreline, seeking the ideal spot for his headquarters. He chose a broad, flat valley north of Whaler's Cove where his waterworks and anchorage were. Here a fine creek flowed year round from the wooded glen past the ancient midden where he built his one-room adobe *hacienda* (on present Pine Street between Caledonia and Bonita). From here he had easier access to his planned cattle empire than in the confined cove. Also, along the flat beach that would later become Caledonia Street, there was plenty of room to set up a second waterworks. He constructed a wharf from the beach out to deeper water, presumably to load cattle hides onto lighters. He slowly expanded his commercial empire and his influence. A map drawn by Eugene Duflot de Mofras in 1841 shows the bay off Sausalito referred to not by the old Spanish name, *Enseña de la Carmelita,* but for the first time, simply, as *Richardson's Bay.*

But change in those days still came slowly to pastoral *Alta California.* Richardson worked at his Sausalito farm, as he called it, aided by his Indian servants and his sons. Estaban, or Steven, born in 1831 at San Gabriel, spent his boyhood years at *Rancho del Sausalito,* speaking Spanish as his native language. He was raised in the saddle, his close friends the sons of other wealthy landowners of the *gente de razón,* or "people who count." His brother Francisco was three years younger and his sister Marianna was the eldest of the children. Sixteen when the family moved to Sausalito, she was by all accounts possessed by the same grace and beauty as her mother. By the time William Richardson had expanded his adobe into a home suitable for *un Patrón Grande,* as he had become, the sons of his many friends were taking a keen interest in Marianna. She became engaged to young Francisco de Haro, who with his brother Ramón and their parents were close friends of the Richardsons.

William Richardson must have known that time was running out for the Arcadian way of life in California. If not, the Bear Flag Revolt of 1846 quickly brought the point home. He learned of the shocking events in Sonoma, where General Vallejo had been imprisoned in his own home, and knew that war was inevitable. John Frémont took command of the ragtag Bearflaggers in Sonoma and was advancing south to capture the Presidio at San Francisco. Stopping at San Rafael with Kit Carson and a collection of soldiers, trappers, and desperadoes, Frémont ordered

*A rare, anonymous painting shows William Richardson's* hacienda *as it appeared* c. 1845. *The pathway along the beach leading to the house would one day become Caledonia Street. The numerous small boats on the beach attest to Richardson's varied activities.*

Richardson to send fresh horses. In response, fifteen-year-old Steven Richardson arrived in San Rafael with some of the horses in time to witness an event that would inflame Mexican sentiment against America for years to come.

The de Haro brothers Francisco and Ramón arrived by boat with their elderly uncle José de los Reyes Berryessa to meet with relatives in San Rafael. As the unarmed trio approached Kit Carson, who was in temporary command in Frémont's absence, Carson ordered his soldiers to fire. They killed Francisco and Ramón instantly, apparently ignoring the old man. The many witnesses, including Steven Richardson, stood frozen with shock as Berryessa, in his grief, pleaded with the Americans to kill him, too. A soldier quickly obliged with a shot to the head.

Word of the incident spread quickly, turning ranchers already suspicious into bitter enemies of the Americans. The few English-speaking landowners like Richardson, John Reed, and Timothy Murphy, all Mexican citizens, were in a difficult position. Frémont apologized with a weak excuse for the killings. Richardson remained aloof as Frémont swept through *Rancho del Sausalito* on his way to the Presidio. Fortunately for Richardson and his neighbors, the bloodiest events of the war with Mexico occurred many hundreds of miles away from Marin.

When hostilities ceased, Richardson and other holders of Mexican land grants awaited their fate at the hands of new masters. Very little changed at first. The vast new American acquisition was ruled by a thin military force commanded by rapidly changing leaders. President Polk, aware of the instability of the situation, directed the military commanders of California to follow established Mexican law and do nothing that could lead to a general rebellion that might in turn lead to foreign intervention. By 1849 as the drive for statehood got under way, the military commander of San Francisco Bay was Colonel Richard Barnes Mason, with Commodore Thomas ap Catesby Jones in charge of the half dozen ships of the Navy's Pacific Squadron. Commodore Jones was well acquainted with Sausalito. His ships were supplied with water there and the anchorage in the cove gave quick access to the bay entrance, or "Golden Gate," as Frémont had christened it.

Jones's problems as Commodore were compounded by the discovery of gold in the hills east of San Francisco. Hundreds of ships, American and foreign, arrived in 1849, straining Jones's resources for keeping order. Thousands of men, crews and passengers, civilian and Navy, left their ships in Yerba Buena Cove and joined the mad scramble for *El Dorado*. The Army and Navy lacked sufficient man-

*Whaling ships in Sausalito's protected cove were a common sight in the years between 1827 and 1850. William Richardson had a ready supply of fresh beef, seasoned lumber, and pure water. These whalers, shown in San Francisco Bay in later years, are almost unchanged from those of Richardson's time. The* Young Phoenix *(right) and* Ocean *(center) are both from New Bedford.*

power to search for deserters; only the most loyal officers could be trusted to go ashore. And even those were tempted when they learned that a lowly civilian laundryman or apprentice carpenter was earning three times the pay of a Navy Lieutenant.

Faced with an unprecedented situation, Commodore Jones wielded his authority in some rather unorthodox ways, stretching and modifying Navy regulations when necessary. It became common for Naval personnel to hire out as civilians in San Francisco where there was a critical shortage of men. To compensate for relatively low pay, Jones allowed his officers to draw rations from government storehouses and board with civilians, using their valuable rations as payment. This came close to violating the constitutional sanction against quartering troops in civilian homes, but of course the Naval officers were more than welcome with their supplies of sugar, coffee, and flour.

During that time, William Richardson was host to a number of officers. At heart always a seafaring man, Richardson felt comfortable with the bold Americans. Naval vessels were held in the cove for long periods, partly to isolate their crews from the gold fever in San Francisco. Officers and men came to   know Sausalito, some to love

it, some to recognize its potential. One of Richardson's guests was Lt. James McCormick, soon to play an important role in Sausalito's fate. McCormick and others were treated to traditional California hospitality; long hunts for grizzly bear and elk, fine meals, music and dancing at the Richardson *hacienda.* They were charmed by Doña Maria Antonia Martinez de Richardson and her daughter Marianna, who with her new husband Manuel Torres lived with the Richardsons. They were among the last to glimpse a way of life soon to vanish.

Not the least of Commodore Jones's problems was the lack of dry dock and repair facilities in California. This was a particular concern for the Navy's newest acquisitions, the *Edith* and the *Massachusetts,* both steam-powered vessels with experimental removable propellers and both subject to frequent breakdowns. While taking on water in the cove, Jones and other officers had observed the potential of Sausalito's flat tidal beach; so in 1849 he established a makeshift dry dock there and put it to a test that summer.

The *Edith,* needing repairs to her propeller shaft, was placed under the temporary command of Lt. McCormick and ordered to the cove. McCormick, using steam power, beached the *Edith* stern first at high tide. The receding tide left the propeller assembly fully exposed and easily repaired. Sausalito was the "only place in California where such repairs could be effected" according to Commodore Jones's report to Washington on the matter. The *Edith* was then ordered to Santa Barbara to pick up the Southern California contingent of delegates to the constitutional convention in Monterey. She sailed from Sausalito on August 20, 1849, and three days later ran aground in a dense fog off Point Conception. Lt. McCormick and the crew escaped injury, but the vessel was a total loss. Lt. McCormick was absolved of any blame for this loss at the official inquiry later at Benicia, Commodore Jones presiding. The Commodore himself, however, became a center of controversy in Washington when several fellow officers criticized his civilian-manned repair facility at Sausalito. The *"Edith* Affair" and subsequent gossip led to a congressional investigation of Jones; as facts came to light, the inquiry broadened into what became known as the "McCormick Affair."

In 1847, even before gold was discovered in California, Commodore Jones had requested the Navy Department in Washington to send a combination sawmill and gristmill around the horn to San Francisco where he needed lumber for ship repairs, and ground flour to feed his sailors. On learning of Jones's request and before his debacle with the *Edith,* Lt. McCormick asked permission to assemble and operate the saw mill, filling Navy requisitions for lumber and selling the lumber remaining on the open market. The Navy rejected his proposal, but shipped the unassembled mill in July, 1848. In November the sawmill and steam

engine parts arrived and were dumped on the beach in Yerba Buena Cove and left scattered about as the ship's crew set off for the gold country. Commodore Jones, still eager to establish a repair facility for his ships, signed a contract with Robert A. Parker, a San Franciscan civilian entrepreneur to assemble and operate the sawmill in the cove at Sausalito. Under terms of the contract, Parker had four months to set up, then three months to operate the mill to recover his start-up costs. Thereafter he must fill Navy requisitions for lumber, not to exceed one-third of the mill capacity. He could then sell the remaining two-thirds at prevailing rates, which since the gold discovery had skyrocketed.

Whether Commodore Jones had Richardson's consent to shift the sawmill site from San Francisco to Sausalito is unrecorded. In all probability Richardson, deeply in debt from borrowing money at horrendous interest rates, welcomed the chance to participate in the frenzy of cash transactions going on around him. In a seemingly unrelated event (at least to the Navy in Washington), Richardson sold some 160 acres of his Rancho Sausalito to Charles Tyler Botts of San Francisco for $35,000 in gold on April 16, 1849.

Commodore Jones meanwhile informed Washington of his sawmill contract with Robert Parker, assuring the Navy there need be no concern over the Sausalito location; he explained that "the ground upon which the mill stands is within fifty *varas* [137½ feet] of high water mark, which according to Mexican law still in effect may be claimed by the government (now the U.S. government) for its use whenever required." The Navy disavowed Jones's right to enter into a contract with a civilian and declared it void, ordering Jones to reclaim the sawmill and settle accounts with Parker for his expenses to date. But Robert Parker had assigned the contract to none other than Lt. James McCormick, who, after the loss of the *Edith,* had become superintendent of the Sausalito sawmill and was drawing a salary of $2,500 a year while still on active duty with the Navy.

Slowly, the Navy Department pieced together the whole story of the troublesome sawmill in the unknown little cove that they referred in dispatches to as "*San*celito." Like so many instant towns that had sprung up during the gold rush wherever a speculator could get a large enough parcel to subdivide into lots, Sausalito had been hastily conceived, with a Navy sawmill as its big attraction. If the founders of Sausalito could have had their way, Sausalito and not Mare Island would have become the Navy base for the Pacific Coast, with dry docks, shipyards, and a fleet anchored in Richardson's Bay.

Navy surveyor Lt. George F. Emmons laid out the town with streets like points on a mariner's compass; it was bounded by North, West, and South streets, with Front Street along the beach. Lots went for $500 each at the high point of sawmill operations in 1850. Lots were eagerly purchased by naval officers who had heard of the action in Sausalito. Lt. Emmons was given a lot in exchange for his services. Captain Leonard Story purchased a lot and built one of the first homes in Sausalito (near

---

A firsthand glimpse of life at William Richardson's *Rancho del Sausalito* survives in the form of a letter written by J. Cowdrey to his brother in 1850. Cowdrey had come to California seeking his fortune, and like so many others was unsuccessful. By November, 1850, circumstances found him in the place he called "South Salito," working for "Don Emanuel," or Manuel Torres, William Richardson's son-in-law.

*"Dear Brother,*

*"It will doubtless appear strange to you to receive a letter dated from this place from me, but strange things happen. I am cooking for a Spanish gentleman whose name is* Don Emanuel, *rich as mud—his farm is twenty one miles long, and from three to nine wide. I have to cook for him and his wife [Marianna Richardson Torres], and from three to a dozen Indians, and at the present time four carpenters, who are at work repairing his house. I wish I was a good carpenter, they get ten dollars per day. In my present situation I have a good deal to do, though when the carpenters are gone it will be easy. Don Emanuel says I am a very good cook. It would astonish you to see how I use up the Beef Creatures. I cook almost a quarter [of beef] a day. I have a fresh quarter every day besides birds. I cook beefsteaks every morning and night—for dinner roast beef and soup, bird stews and puddings—then I have bread to make. I have a little Indian boy to wait on me. They eat no cold meat here at all— what is left from the table is given to the Indians to eat what they have a mind to, the balance thrown away, which amounts to half a barrel a day. I am learning to talk Spanish quite fast. I think if I stay here two months I shall get so as to talk very good Spanish."*

Richardson and Second streets). The names of investors read like a Navy roll call: Captains Charles Lauff and T. F. Peck, as well as Captain Coffin and Captain George Snow and engineers James Boyd and William Mercier. Several were civilians at heart who had enlisted in the Navy in order to get to California. Rodman Price, who returned to New Jersey in 1858 to become Governor, had been purser on the *Cyane,* served in the Mexican War, and resigned in December, 1850. William Carrington who had been an assistant surgeon resigned September, 1851. Botts had arrived in California as Navy storekeeper on the *Matilda* in 1848. Even Commodore Thomas ap Catesby Jones purchased a lot. And of course none other than Lt. James McCormick owned the key lots next to the creek outflow at the foot of Main Street, known as the "fountain."

There he built a hotel or rooming house called the "Fountain House." Between Second and Third streets he built a ten-pin alley in a small house for the amusement of sailors from ships anchored in the cove. Sausalito's first hotel was probably the "Saucelito House," built around 1849 from lumber cut at the sawmill. Capt. George Snow ran this establishment, which lasted until 1875.

Robert Parker dropped out of the picture in Sausalito, perhaps because his main interest, the gristmill, never materialized or was stolen from the beach in Yerba Buena. In any case, during the gold rush, Parker was busy with his grocery and liquor business in San Francisco. There

he also ran the "Parker House," where in 1851 he was charging $1,500 a month for a room.

The sawmill operation in Sausalito, a cluster of buildings on the creek running approximately down Main Street at Third, consisted of a government storehouse, the mill building, and several small sheds and shanties for the crew. The mill did a brisk business in 1850, selling pine planks and assorted redwood lumber to the Navy as well as to ranchers and builders. Even William Richardson bought lumber from the mill and in turn sold beef to McCormick for his sawmill crew, many of whom were moonlighting sailors. Even so, the mill never lived up to expectations. During the winters it was more difficult than had been anticipated to fell redwoods beyond Corte Madera Creek and raft the logs down Richardson's Bay to the cove.

Finally in 1851 the Navy demanded that the mill be seized from McCormick and sold at auction. McCormick made a detailed accounting of his and Parker's expenses and receipts. Referees for the Navy and McCormick's attorney Charles Botts concluded that McCormick was owed $25,766.64 to cover the difference between his costs and revenue from the mill.

The Navy refused payment, not surprisingly, since McCormick had listed among other expenses payments to navy personnel for loading navy lumber onto navy vessels in Sausalito. The dispute over the $25,000 shifted from Sausalito to Washington, D.C. in 1851 when the "McCor-

---

In 1862 a traveller passed through what was left of Charles Botts's "Old Saucelito." William Henry Brewer recorded in his diary observations of what must have been Captain George Snow's "Saucelito House," built in 1849 and burned in 1875.

Wednesday, March 26, 1862

"... It was long after dark before we found Sausalito where we stopped at an Irish hotel. We ate a hearty supper, then sat in the kitchen and talked.

"Hogarth never sketched such a scene as that. The kitchen with furniture scattered around, driftwood in the corners, salt fish hanging to the ceilings and walls, lanterns, old ship furniture, fishing and boating apparatus, Spanish saddle and *riata* — but I can't enumerate all. Well, we stayed there all night and for several hours the next morning, then took a small boat for San Francisco along with a load of calves and pigs piled in the bottom."

Brewer also couldn't resist a dig at Sausalito in general:

"Sausalito is a place of half a dozen houses once destined to be a great town ... $150,000 lost there; City laid out, corner lots sold at enormous prices, 'water fronts' still higher ... for a big city was bound to grow up there and then these lots would be worth money. The old California story, everybody bought land to rise in value but no one built. No city grew there. Half a dozen huts and shanties mark the place and 'corner lots' and 'water fronts' are alike valueless."

*The earliest-known photograph of Sausalito, c. 1852, shows Charles Botts's metropolis at its zenith, with perhaps thirty inhabitants. The "Saucelito House" stands in the center of the little cluster of buildings where Second and Main are today.*

mick Case" went before Congress. Rep. Jonathon Minor Botts of Virginia, brother of Charles Botts, owner of old Sausalito, had a bill introduced to appropriate $25,000 as a settlement to McCormick for the sawmill operation.

The Navy announced in 1852 that the site for a new Navy Yard on the West Coast would be Mare Island. A study had been conducted by Commodore McCauley, who had replaced Commodore Jones in 1851, to find the most eligible site for the naval arsenal and dry dock. McCauley, like Jones before him, recommended Sausalito. But other forces were at work. A group of enterprising men, with the support of General Mariano Vallejo, promoted Mare Island, the site next to the new town named by Vallejo's son-in-law John B. Frisbee in honor of the General. Mare Island was selected, possibly because of the cloud of doubt raised over Sausalito by the conduct of certain Naval officers. Officially it was chosen because of its deep channel and its strategic distance from the Golden Gate.

Charles Botts continued to sell lots in Sausalito, being careful to retain water rights on the property. Even if the dry dock deal fell through, he could at least continue with a water company that might prove profitable.

With construction proceeding apace in San Francisco and other towns around the bay, milled lumber was a scarce commodity. Devastating fires that were all too common added to the lumber shortage. On November 2, 1852,

one such fire broke out in Sacramento, racing unchecked through wood frame buildings along the river front until over 1,600 buildings were destroyed—almost two-thirds of the town. Undaunted, optimistic merchants began immediately to rebuild. Wooden buildings in other towns were actually dismantled and shipped to Sacramento where lumber brought an exorbitant price. Seizing an opportunity, the few settlers left in Sausalito sold their buildings, lock, stock, and last barrel. All but vestiges of Richardson's dream of a metropolis in Sausalito sailed away up the Sacramento River. The mill remained, also Captain Story's house, several shanties, and the "Saucelito House." For the next twenty years as San Francisco grew to become a major city with over 100,000 inhabitants, "Old Saucelito" lay dormant, a peaceful little cove visited only by crews of vessels anchored in Richardson's Bay.

William Richardson still had reaped no profits from the gold rush. Unwilling to leave his fragile "empire" for the goldfields, he also forbade his son to venture to the dangerous mining camps. His hope for riches lay in somehow turning his *Rancho del Sausalito* to advantage. He became preoccupied with proving his Mexican grant before the United States Land Claims Commission in San Francisco. During this period his cattle business went untended, and his merchant vessels had new, fierce competition. Richardson also had an unfortunate but not uncommon habit of borrowing short-term money at high

*San Francisco in early 1853, with Yerba Buena Island in the background. By this time San Francisco's population had reached 50,000, thanks to the gold rush.*

11

*Charles Tyler Botts, in San Francisco around 1849. William Richardson always dreamed of a city that would spring up in Sausalito. Charles Botts actually did something about it. Botts, born in 1809, son of a prominent Virginia lawyer, came to California with his wife Margaret in 1848 on the ship* Matilda. *He became the naval storekeeper in Monterey, a position of considerable influence and prestige. During the gold rush, he set up law offices in San Francisco. Always a stylish dresser, he seems here to be in the garb of a sourdough (which he never was).*

*Botts raised $35,000 in gold to purchase 160 acres in Sausalito's cove from financially desperate William Richardson in 1849. Botts was also a delegate to the California Constitutional Convention that same year, where he was one of the more vocal participants.*

*After Mare Island was selected as the United States Navy shipyard for the West Coast, Botts lost interest in his Sausalito real-estate venture and sold his remaining property to others. In 1858 he moved to Sacramento where he tried his hand in the newspaper business and also became a judge in Yolo County. During the Civil War, Botts returned briefly to Virginia. In 1865, back in California, he set up a law office once more in San Francisco and moved with his wife and daughter to Oakland. In the 1870s he was a highly respected attorney and judge in the East Bay. Charles Tyler Botts died in San Francisco, October 4, 1884. His thoughts on Sausalito's progress to that time are unfortunately unrecorded.*

interest rates to cover debts. Unable to pay off one debt, he borrowed more, usually from friends, each time using his vast property as collateral. It is unknown how many times he did this, but for years after his death unrecorded promissory notes surfaced, each bearing Richardson's signature, each naming *Rancho del Sausalito* as collateral.

Still heavily mortgaged in the mid-1850s, Richardson was forced to liquidate his assets in a last attempt to salvage his ranch. His attorney, after successfully clearing Richardson's land claim, directed him to Samuel Reading Throckmorton, an attorney well known for his clever financial manipulations. Richardson and Throckmorton struck a deal wherein Throckmorton was given title as trustee to the entire remaining *Rancho del Sausalito*. He would have three years in which to raise money by selling off parts of the ranch to cover all debts. At that time he would deed back to Richardson one-fifth of all remaining unencumbered property and assets, keeping four-fifths for himself as payment for his efforts. In addition to the cove, which he had sold to Charles Botts in 1849, Richardson had already deeded 640 prime acres of the ranch to his wife and children (most of New Town today), and he had managed to keep that parcel unmortgaged. That land, plus the one-fifth share he would get back from Throckmorton would more than provide for his family's security.

Throckmorton immediately restructured the ranch from a stock range to dairying, a more profitable business at the time. In 1856 the final blow came for William Richardson. Three of his uninsured coastal vessels, the backbone of his financial base, were lost at sea. Bankrupt, discouraged, and threatened with lawsuits, William Antonio Richardson died April 20, 1856, allegedly of mercury poisoning from tablets prescribed by his doctor for rheumatism. Accidental or intentional, his death at age sixty-one remains one final mystery in his enigmatic life.

Although the three years allotted to Throckmorton to untangle Richardson's financial snarl had already elapsed, Throckmorton waited until after Richardson's death to report on his progress. He met with twenty-four-year-old Steven Richardson and Manuel Torres, Richardson's son-in-law, and told them a sad tale. *Rancho del Sausalito* was deeper in debt than ever, and the one-fifth promised them was in reality one-fifth of nothing but enormous debts. Under terms of the agreement, the entire property, debts and all, should have reverted to Richardson's heirs. But the resourceful Throckmorton had a proposal. According to Steven Richardson, Throckmorton offered him and Torres $5,000 each for the family's one-fifth share, which of course was "worthless" anyway. Like lambs to the slaughter, they signed over their interests to Throckmorton

without even asking for an accounting of debts. It turned out the total indebtedness was far less than they had been led to believe. As Steven Richardson said in retrospect, "He [Throckmorton] was dealing with a pair of suckers. Thus we parted with a principality for a beggarly pittance."

Now with complete control of *Rancho del Sausalito,* except for Maria Richardson's 640 acres and Charles Botts's "Old Saucelito," Throckmorton, also now in debt, set out to turn a profit. He first tried to sell off Lime Point, the Golden Gate headlands, to the U.S. government as a military preserve. The Army had been interested in the headlands since 1854 when it had first approached William Richardson, but his asking price of $400,000 was too steep, even for the government. Now it entered into long negotiations with Throckmorton for the property. Finally, in 1866, Lime Point Tract was sold to the military for $125,000. This 1,889-acre parcel would become Fort Baker, and would fix the southern and western boundaries of Sausalito.

Two years later Throckmorton put together the real estate deal of a lifetime. He learned of the sale of Maria Richardson's 640-acre parcel, including the family *hacienda,* to speculators John H. Turney and his partner James Boyd. By joining forces with them, Throckmorton was able to offer a complete package to potential investors: a choice valley with long, flat shoreline, and excellent springs and creeks. On April 22, 1868, they sold 1,164 acres of the Sausalito rancho to a consortium of nineteen San Francisco businessmen for $440,000.

The partners in the new Sausalito venture formally incorporated on September 27, 1869, as the Sausalito Land & Ferry Company, thus launching the second attempt to create a city in Sausalito. Some of the partners were interested in the quick profit potential, while others, like Charles Harrison, were dedicated to the idea of founding a town. (A complete list of partners in Sausalito Land & Ferry Company is on page 181.) Maurice Dore, one partner, was a successful, respected land broker and auctioneer in San Francisco. He was a close friend of William C. Ralston of the Bank of California and had a firmly established reputation in the San Francisco banking community. It was Dore perhaps more than any other who gave the group credibility, and who worked out the complicated land transaction with Throckmorton.

*The* Princess *was launched September 14, 1858, destined for a career on the Sacramento River. Designed to haul freight and a few passengers for Coffey and Risdon, she was 130 feet long with a 21-foot beam and twin 18-foot paddle wheels. The* Princess *was purchased by the Sausalito Land & Ferry Company just days before her inaugural voyage as a ferryboat on May 10, 1868. She made two trips a day from the Princess Street landing to Meigg's Wharf in San Francisco. Soon after she began service, her wheel house was raised for better visibility to the position shown in the painting. When the North Pacific Coast Railroad took over ferry operations in 1875, the* Princess *was sold and five years later was broken up for scrap.*

*Thomas Wosser, first engineer on the ferryboat* Princess *and first of five generations of Wossers who served on ferryboats. He was born in Ireland in 1828 and came to San Francisco around Cape Horn in 1849. Hired as a boatman by Charles Harrison in 1851, he remained in that capacity until his retirement in 1896. He built one of the first homes in New Town, where he lived with his wife and fourteen children until his death in 1900. The house, which stands today, was occupied by the Wosser family until 1981.*

The Sausalito Land & Ferry Company set to work soon after the land was purchased. They had a survey made and a map drawn up showing future streets and lots available to the public. They named the streets mainly in honor of themselves and quickly staked out prime lots for their *villas* overlooking Richardson's Bay. They sent one of their number, John L. Romer, off to purchase a ferryboat.

The first streets graded and opened for business were a section of Water Street and Princess Street, named for the little steamer the company had purchased. This area was envisioned as the hub of a business district, with residences to be built on the view lots.

*"New" Sausalito from the North Pacific Coast Railroad wharf, looking south c. 1875. In this photo by English photographer Edward Muybridge, the man perched on the new wharf gazes back at the first ferry landing at the foot of Princess Street. The ferryboat* Princess *rests at her pier and Greene's Hotel appears at center.*

The Bower was built in 1869 on one of the first lots sold by the Sausalito Land & Ferry Company. Builder and original resident was former South Carolina Senator James H. Gardner, shown mounted on his horse "Dick." The Bower for many years was also the home of George H. Harlan Sr., grandson of Mrs. James Gardner.

The Bower today.

The new town almost suffered the same fate as Charles Botts's "Old Saucelito" venture. The company struggled into the seventies with infusions of cash by the partners, who strained their lines of credit in San Francisco's financial community. Although a few lots were sold and a few homes were built, people were not flocking to the new utopia as had been hoped. Small hotels were built near the ferry landing so that potential customers might have a leisurely look at the properties and experience the sublime climate and serenity of Sausalito.

Samuel Throckmorton tried to foreclose on the Sausalito Land & Ferry Company several times, but each time the determined businessmen successfully evaded the hammer. At one desperate point, in order to raise money, they transferred all the remaining property to Maurice Dore for one dollar. Dore, whose land auction business had prospered, was the only one whose credit was still good. The company held auctions from time to time, trying to drum up enthusiasm for Sausalito lots, but they were competing with cheap land in many new towns around the Bay Area, many with railroad connections. In an effort to lure newcomers with capital, every new town around San Francisco Bay was promising prosperity, healthful climates, rapid growth, and boundless opportunity.

Still the prospects looked good to the men of the Sausalito Land & Ferry Company. Completion of the transcontinental railroad in 1869 injected new vitality into California, and San Francisco had become the financial center of the West. The Pacific Mail Steamship Company had established regular routes to the Orient from San Francisco, and a thriving California grain trade filled the bay with ships from Liverpool and New England.

As grain ships were laid up in Carquinez Strait and Richardson's Bay waiting for the grain to be harvested or for the price to go up in home ports, their masters and crews became enamored of life in California. Many of the earliest settlers in Sausalito were British, who perhaps preferred the quiet country life to that of dynamic, raw San Francisco. Some were sent to represent British companies, some came from the vessels themselves. Others came to seek their fortunes in the legendary land of California. Most of the English residents of Sausalito were "second sons." That is, they came from landed wealthy English families and although they usually had sufficient annual stipends, they had no titles. The eldest son stood to inherit the title and property in England, leaving the other sons and daughters to seek their fortunes elsewhere. The men took positions in banking and brokerage houses, and the women often married American businessmen.

*Madrona Cottage today.*

*John L. Romer, who had purchased the ferryboat* Princess *on behalf of the Sausalito Land & Ferry Company built Madrona Cottage in 1874 as a wedding present for his daughter, Mrs. William Ritchie. This house was beautifully restored in 1977.*

17

*Engine Number One, the* Saucelito *was a Baldwin eight-wheeler. She is shown here in service with the White Lumber Company c. 1880.*

At last on April 12, 1873, an event occurred that seemed to secure Sausalito's future. Amid much enthusiastic cheering, a groundbreaking ceremony took place in Sausalito, marking the start of construction of the long-promised railroad that would link Sausalito to the lumber empire to the north.

Railroads were the key to growth for towns all over the country, and California was no exception. New towns struggling for existence suddenly prospered when even the thinnest of rail links was established. San Rafael was one of the first to have its own line, the San Rafael and San Quentin Railroad. This single broad-gauge track between the ferry landing at Point San Quentin and the center of San Rafael gave an invigorating boost to local commerce.

The North Pacific Coast Railroad, incorporated in 1871 with the aid of a public bond issue in Marin County, had a grand plan to run a line through Marin connecting the emerging towns, and continuing up the coast to the vast redwood stands along the Russian River in Sonoma and the Gualala River in Mendocino County. The Sausalito Land & Ferry Company directors, sensing that this could be the breakthrough for their town, gave the financially feeble railroad company thirty acres along Sausalito's

waterfront as an inducement to make Sausalito the southern terminus of the new line.

Because the bond issue called for a southern terminus at Point San Quentin rather than at Sausalito, a legal battle ensued. After considerable legal fireworks, Sausalito won out, and in 1873 construction began. One work gang commenced at Tomales, moving south. Another gang worked at Fairfax, and a third started at Strawberry Point where a trestle was constructed across Richardson's Bay to Sausalito. The trestle connected with Alameda Point (later Pine Station), approximately where Nevada Street meets Bridgeway today.

North Pacific Coast Locomotive Number One "Saucelito" was shipped by sea to Tomales in 1874 as work progressed on the rails. Ambition being tempered by the lack of cold cash, it was decided that Tomales would be the northern terminus for the time being. On January 7, 1875, another ceremony marked the passing of the first train over the completed line. James Wilkins, a former mayor of San Rafael and founder of the *Sausalito News,* recalled in 1927: "The railroad, as completed in 1875, was a ramshackle narrow gauge affair, built along the lines of least resistance, with a lofty disdain of the laws of gravity and a preference for curvature instead of tangents."

*Logs were also transported to mills in San Francisco directly from Ross Landing at Corte Madera Creek, shown here in 1875, the year the first NPCRR trains rolled into Sausalito. In this photo by Muybridge, cordwood is loaded on a small, unidentified schooner.*

*Steam lumber schooners were in direct competition with the railroad. Usually operated by lumber companies, the small steamers worked the "dog hole" ports along the coast. The steam schooner* Newsboy, *shown here at Fort Bragg, was built in 1888 in San Francisco and was the first ship owned by Robert Dollar, founder of the Dollar Steamship Line.*
Newsboy *became a familiar sight in Sausalito around 1900 when she would pick up lumber bound for southern ports like San Diego from the railroad wharf.*

19

*Turney Valley (New Town), looking north c. 1880. This view contrasts to the painting of the same scene on page 7, and shows the impact of the railroad on Sausalito. Caledonia Street runs from the foreground towards Hannon's Hill near Napa Street. In the background is the railroad trestle crossing Richardson's Bay from Pine Point to Strawberry Point. At the left middle is the long, one-story white adobe once the home of William Richardson. As it does today, Mount Tamalpais provides a backdrop to the scene.*

The Sausalito Land & Ferry Company retired the nineteen-year-old ferryboat *Princess* and happily turned over all ferry operations to the railroad. A new ferry landing and railroad wharf was built slightly north of the old one at Princess Street. There it would remain for the next sixty-six years. Trains began hauling logs and lumber from the redwood forests to feed San Francisco's endless building boom. And passengers came too, commuters from fledgling towns along the line and vacationers from San Francisco. Sausalito's small business community was delighted and encouraged by the influx of new people as shops and stores opened for business along Caledonia Street near William Richardson's old *casa*.

In the summer of 1875, the North Pacific Coast Railroad absorbed the San Rafael and San Quentin Railroad and converted it to narrow gauge from broad gauge to unify the two lines. The main passenger terminal was shifted from Sausalito to Point San Quentin, where it would remain until 1884. Even though the wharf remained in Sausalito, and several trains a day brought passengers and dairy products from nearby towns, the main traffic was routed through San Quentin. The track from San Rafael to San Quentin avoided the several steep grades and curves on the line to Sausalito.

In spite of that setback, Sausalito continued to grow. With the railroad came more people, laborers at first, then merchants from many national backgrounds. Added to the Americans and British were families from Italy, France, Germany, Austria, and Portugal, from China, Ireland, and Greece— all contributing to the character of Sausalito. The racist overtones of the era, in particular the anti-Chinese mood of the country, left its mark in Sausalito. The Chinese railroad workers who stayed in Sausalito were confined to "Shanghai Valley," near Spring Street.

20

*The Sausalito railroad and ferry wharf in 1888 demonstrates how the business district was built up around the new terminal after the Princess Street landing was abandoned in 1875. The large building on Water Street just above the train is the Tamalpais Hotel, with the Lisbon Hotel next door. On the hill above the Tamalpais is the Casa Madrona. The sign on the barn at left center reads: "Building Lots and Villa Sites adjoining P.Y.C. [Pacific Yacht Club] Grounds at Auction, Saturday, 12th May, 1888."*

About 100 in number, the Chinese suffered through the first winter, when 25 died from an unrecorded disease. After the railroad was completed, the small group, mostly families, raised potatoes and other vegetables for sale. Still unwelcome in Sausalito, they soon moved on. Once the wave of fear and prejudice passed, Chinese shrimp fishermen and merchants slowly came back to Sausalito, although even in the 1890s most Chinese and Japanese in Sausalito were household servants.

*Painting by Norton Bush looking north, after 1884. The railroad trestle across Richardson's Bay has been abandoned, and tracks now run straight from the Sausalito terminal past Pine Point to Waldo Point, shown in the painting just ahead of the locomotive.*

The North Pacific Coast Railroad purchased ferries to replace the *Princess* and to add to the San Quentin run to assist the *Clinton* and *Contra Costa.* The steamer *Petaluma* was acquired and renamed the *Petaluma of Saucelito* (later renamed *Tamalpais*). Two new, more elegant ferries were ordered: the *San Rafael* and the *Saucelito.* But by 1880 the free spending of the railroad had taken a heavy toll. A deep economic recession in the late 1870s, triggered by the collapse of the New York banking firm, Jay Cooke & Company, affected many heavily indebted business ventures, including both the Sausalito Land & Ferry Company and the railroad. Creditors foreclosed in 1880 on the North Pacific Coast Railroad, and it was forced to sell.

A newly capitalized company calling itself the North Pacific Coast Extension Company was formed with plans for a more direct route from Sausalito north. New tracks were laid on a causeway straight across the salt marshes from the Sausalito terminal to Alameda Point, then straight across to Waldo Point (above). In 1884 the Richardson's Bay trestle was abandoned and San Quentin ferry service discontinued. But in spite of continued financial difficulties, the railroad expanded and absorbed smaller lines until it reached Cazadero in the north.

The railroad brought not only working class and merchant class newcomers to Sausalito but also wealthy entrepreneurs, who usually took up residence in one of several new hotels.

*Initial success of the North Pacific Coast Railroad led to purchase of two large ferryboats, the* San Rafael *and the* Saucelito *in 1877.* San Rafael *pictured here, was prefabricated in New York and carried west on 120 rail cars where she was reassembled at the Union Iron Works in San Francisco. Built in the grand Victorian manner, she had elaborate hardwood carving and red plush seats in her main salon. An unusual feature, common on East Coast steamers of the period, were the overhead trusses, port and starboard, running the length of the superstructure. With her enormous paddle boxes, the* San Rafael *was a familiar sight on San Francisco Bay for over twenty years.*

*The* Saucelito, *also prefabricated in New York, was identical to the* San Rafael *except for an octagonal wheel house rather than a round one. Under the command of Captain Brooks, the* Saucelito *caught fire while tied to the San Quentin ferry landing on February 24, 1884. Both the vessel and the dock were totally destroyed; thus Sausalito became once again the primary terminus of the North Pacific Coast Railroad. The* San Rafael *came to a tragic end also when she was struck by the ferryboat* Sausalito *(built in 1894), in a dense fog off Alcatraz on November 30, 1901. The two vessels were lashed together long enough for more than 200 passengers aboard the doomed* San Rafael *to be transferred to the* Sausalito. *At least two men were lost as well as the horse "Old Dick" kept on the* San Rafael *to haul express carts. The dramatic sinking inspired Jack London to create a similar scene in his 1904 novel,* The Sea Wolf.

23

One of the oldest and most widely known hotels in Sausalito was the El Monte, shown here in an anonymous watercolor painting done about 1882. Below the imposing three-story Victorian edifice on Bulkley Avenue is the railroad wharf and the ferryboat *Petaluma of Saucelito,* later renamed the *Tamalpais.* The El Monte began its hotel life as the Bon Ton around 1878, although parts of the structure may have been built prior to 1869. It was like many grand hotels of the era, catering to the wealthy class with accommodations for servants in adjoining small rooms. The suites were designed to encourage lengthy stays, and the management frowned on overnight guests. But like many "wooden palaces" of that time, the Bon Ton struggled financially while keeping up a facade of gracious standards for the likes of Claus Spreckels, the Crockers, and Robert Dollar. Under different managements over the years, the hotel was called the Clifton House, the El Monte, the Terrace, and the Geneva Hotel, and became a boarding house shortly before it was demolished in 1904.

It was under the ownership of Australian John E. Slinkey that the hotel, then known as the El Monte, acquired its greatest fame. Slinkey may not have lived up to his name literally, but he was crafty and energetic. He had a hand in almost everything that happened in Sausalito in the 1880s, and his El Monte was a gathering place for political and social groups. The guest list read like a Who's Who of San Francisco, and Slinkey catered to the guest's every whim. He even installed a bowling alley exclusively for the use of ladies. Many British and other visitors stayed at the El Monte as the first step to becoming permanent Sausalito residents.

*The Ammerman residence on Miller Lane was originally known as a "bachelor house," one of several Sausalito homes where single young gentlemen could find lodgings. Single young ladies stayed with family friends and relatives upon arrival in Sausalito, and were introduced to eligible bachelors through one of the numerous church and social events.*

*Typical of many young men from England, this lad whose name is unrecorded left his ship and took up permanant residence in Sausalito in the 1880s.*

These British merchant-class homeowners in Sausalito and their wives set the social style of Sausalito. The British Benevolent Society (the first of many such ethnic organizations), open to all those born under the Union Jack, was formed in San Francisco in 1865, and by the early 1870s Sausalito was well represented in the society.

Rebecca Dixon Chambers, a long-time Sausalito resident, recalled the town's earlier days. Although her recollections were of the turn of the century, they applied in many respects to the 1870s. "When the Dixons moved to Sausalito, it was still an unspoiled British colony. There were more British people on the hill than Americans. The English crowd worked together, and the American crowd had their set. They mingled in a friendly way, but the English set the tone and quality of general life, informal and natural; but when there was a formal party, it was properly conducted."

Christ Church, at Santa Rosa and San Carlos Avenues was built in 1882 and is the oldest surviving church structure in Sausalito. Even though the hilltop location has become abundant with trees, anyone familiar with the church today would instantly recognize it in this 1887 photograph. The porch and entry were moved to align with the center aisle in 1913, and the bell tower has been slightly modified.

The "Flirtation Group" (left), in 1885. It is noted that the group, perhaps about to be off on a picnic, is chaperoned by Mrs. Q. T. Marvin standing at right. The gentleman in clerical garb and the straw boater is the Rev. Frederick W. Reed, first rector of Christ Church, gazing fondly at his wife to be, Miss Ella Avery. The heavy British flavor of Sausalito's early days is evident here. The names of the rest of the group are very English: May Merry, Blanch Merry, Etta Barrett, Sallie Maynard, Robert Maynard, Charles Barrett, Kate Stone, and Claude Hamilton.

*The painting above by Norton Bush shows a quiet Sausalito Sunday morning in 1885. The bell tower of Christ Church is at lower left, and Paul Fleury's residence, Mira Mar, stands prominently at center. Captains and their families in ships at anchor in Richardson's Bay could row ashore to attend services.*

*Christ Church, 1983*

The first church in Sausalito was the Methodist Church built in 1872 on Hannon's Hill (above Caledonia and Napa Streets). The little building, a private home today, was used only occasionally since Marin County's sparse population meant most ministries covered many miles. About that same time Anglican Sunday services were held in Sausalito for the many British residents. By 1878 plans were under way to construct an Episcopal church on the hill above Richardson's Bay. An attempt was made in 1877 to organize a Catholic congregation in Sausalito, and a parish was successfully established in 1881. The churches became mainstays of Sausalito social order and to this day figure prominently in the town's cohesiveness and sense of civic pride.

*This sturdy American Gothic edifice was Sausalito's first Catholic church, completed in 1881. Saint Mary, Star of the Sea stood at Litho and Bonita Streets in New Town, and was demolished in 1920 after only forty years' service. A second Catholic church, Holy Family Hall, was constructed in Old Town in 1908, but it was destroyed in the fire of 1919 as a third church was nearing completion. The new, bigger structure, also called Saint Mary, Star of the Sea, was built on the site of Hamlin's villa* La Vuelta *on Harrison Avenue.*

In early December, 1909, a train pulled into the Sausalito depot bearing a special cargo. Two large bells were unloaded, each weighing 1,500 pounds, each cast in copper and tin and tuned to the key of "G." Carried overland by rail from the foundry in Missouri, they were to become proud additions to Sausalito's Catholic churches, Saint Mary, Star of the Sea and Holy Family Church in Old Town.

The bells were christened on December 12, 1909, by Father John Valentini, in a solemn ceremony recalled for years after in the community as "the blessing of the bells." Each bell bore a different inscription and each had its own godparents. "Virginia," named by godparents Mr. and Mrs. Michael Hannon, prominent Sausalito residents for some thirty years, was installed in the bell tower at Star of the Sea Church. The inscription read: VIRGINIA G., To St. Mary, Star of the Sea Church, Sausalito, 1909.

"Edward" was named by godparents Mrs. E. L. Auzerais and Mr. William Alexander Coulter, the noted marine artist. The gleaming surface of "Edward" carried the inscription: In Memory of Edward Auzerais, to Holy Family Church, Sausalito, 1909.

The bells began their days of service ringing in Christmas Eve that same year, 1909. At the Star of the Sea Church, installation of the new bell triggered a second historic event: the removal of the Old Mission bell, which had been on loan from Mission San Rafael since 1880. The old bell was gratefully returned to the mission.

The roaring fire that swept through Hurricane Gulch in September, 1919, consumed many of the wooden structures of Old Town, including the Holy Family Church on Third Street. As to the fate of "Edward," no record has ever been found. In all probability it was destroyed in the fire.

"Virginia," however, can be seen to this day outside St. Mary's (the newest Catholic Church in Sausalito) on Harrison Avenue. It stands as the sole survivor of "the blessing of the bells" that distant day in 1909, when a speaker is reported to have declared with more optimism than most of us feel today, "May the vibrations of these blessed bells drive out wicked spirits, wicked lives, evil doers!"

*First Presbyterian Church today.*

CHRISTIANSEN

*Another gem of church architecture in Sausalito is the First Presbyterian Church on Bulkley Avenue built in 1909. The First Presbyterian Church was established in 1902, growing out of a remnant of the First Congregational Church organized in 1891. The brown shingle structure designed by Ernest Coxhead is often thought to be the work of Bernard Maybeck, who worked for Coxhead for a time. The property on which the church stands was donated by L. M. Hickman in 1904 after he acquired the lots at auction. Originally it had been part of the El Monte Hotel grounds, subdivided when the old hotel was demolished that same year.*

*Chamarita procession on Filbert Avenue, c. 1900.*

*Chamarita procession leaving St. Mary, Star of the Sea Church, c. 1920.*

*Turney Valley, 1910.*

*T*urney Valley in New Town (above) in 1910 was home to many of Sausalito's Portuguese families. Saint Mary, Star of the Sea Church, in the center foreground was the focal point of the annual Festival of the Holy Ghost. The Portuguese community's observance of the festival on Pentecost Sunday is based on an event in the late thirteenth century. Queen Isabel of Portugal prayed to the Holy Ghost to end the two-year famine that wracked her country and her prayers were answered. A celebration was held that has been reinacted each year since. A feast symbolic of the end of famine is a central part of the festival. The traditional meal consists of *Sopa, Carne e Vino* (soup, meat, and wine) following Mass, and a procession through Sausalito streets proclaiming the visit by the Holy Ghost.

When the first Portuguese immigrants came to California from the Azores Islands in the 1880s, they brought the tradition of the festival with them. It has been perpetuated through a Portuguese fraternal organization, *Irmandade Do Divino Espirito Santo E Da Santissima Trinidade* — The Brotherhood of the Holy Ghost and Blessed Trinity, commonly called I.D.E.S.S.T. The Festival of the Holy Ghost began in Sausalito in 1887 and in the early years lasted up to two weeks. Portuguese parishioners came to Sausalito from isolated dairy farms and small towns in Marin and elsewhere making the event a warm "gathering of the clan." In the evenings there was much music and gaiety as celebrants danced the *Chama Rita,* a traditional folk dance. Sometime after 1900 the entire festival became known as the Chamarita.

Cattle bedecked with flowers were driven through the streets to be blessed by the priest before becoming part of the symbolic feast. The photo at top left shows the procession on Filbert Avenue around 1900. Below it, parishioners are shown leaving the church with young ladies representing Queen Isabel and her attendants. The crown she wears supports a white dove with outstretched wings symbolizing the visit by the Holy Ghost to Queen Isabel in the form of a dove in 1296, marking the end of the famine.

Sausalito's Chamarita Festival continues today in its traditional form. Portuguese families from Marin and Sonoma Counties and as far away as Half Moon Bay come to Sausalito for the event. The festive dancing and symbolic feast are held in I.D.E.S.S.T. Hall on Caledonia Street, built in 1954. Prior to that date the event was held at the Portuguese Hall on Filbert Street, built in 1888. That building today is the First Baptist Church of Sausalito.

The Hill in 1885, with the new Christ Church on the horizon at right. William Ritchie's Cottage Madrona is at lower left. In the center is the treeless Crossroads, the intersection of San Carlos and Harrison Avenues and Glen Drive, then named Lower Santa Rosa Avenue. An almost level trail leads from Turney Valley at the left across unsold lots to Christ Church, providing an easy climb for parishioners' horses on Sunday mornings.

The entry hall at Hazel Mount.

*Charles Henry Harrison at home in Sausalito, in his "Lazy Seat" overlooking Richardson's Bay. Photographed by George Tasheira in 1885 in the gardens at Hazel Mount.*

*As one of the original incorporators of the Sausalito Land & Ferry Company, Harrison claimed the property from Harrison Avenue (named for himself), to San Carlos Avenue down to the intersection of Atwood. In 1869, on this nearly level parcel, he constructed his first modest cottage called Hazel Mount. The Harrisons returned to England for a visit in 1887-89 and had the first Hazel Mount demolished. In its place was built this Norman-English mansion also called Hazel Mount.*

Hollyoaks, the home of Mr. and Mrs. George W. Meade. Built in 1887 on Harrison Avenue, it was perhaps the grandest Victorian home ever built in Sausalito, surpassing even Hazel Mount in ornate splendor. Hollyoaks exemplified fine craftsmanship from enamel-tiled chimneys and lacy, roof ironwork to opulent interiors with imported hardwoods and expensive European furnishings. After the Meades sold Hollyoaks in 1889 for $18,000, the new owners found thirty-five rooms on four floors a bit much to handle and it was converted into a rooming house, finally becoming the Holly Oaks Hotel. In 1939, just before the housing shortage of World War II, Hollyoaks was demolished.

Two magnesium light photographs taken in George Whitney Reed's Sausalito residence, Mossbrae. The time is 10 P.M. on an evening in April, 1888. Mr. Reed (brother of the Rector of Christ Church, Frederick Reed) has composed a self-portrait entitled, "Music Hath Charms."

*On the terrace at Hollyoaks overlooking Richardson's Bay. Then as now a favorite Sausalito pastime.*

*Lily Bronte Reed is captured in a flash of magnesium powder by her husband in a vignette of Victorian daily life he called "My Better Half."*

Top left: Sausalito waterfront and The Hill c. 1885.
Individual water tanks for fire protection and a few wind-
driven water pumps are visible among the fashionable homes
on the hillside.

Top Right: The Hill above the railroad wharf in 1886.
On the ridgeline are (left) the Shoobert House and (right),
Tillinghast's Bungalow. The large white Italianate mansion
below is the Casa Madrona, built in 1885 by William G.
Barrett as a family home. The Casa Madrona, like so many
other mansions when domestic help became an extravagance,
was converted to a boarding house and hotel. In 1960 when
Robert and Marie-Louise Deschamps opened a small but
elegant French restaurant in the building, the Casa Madrona
received widespread fame.

Left: The residence of Mr. and Mrs. William T. Tillinghast
on Harrison Avenue was called The Bungalow. Completed
in 1873, it was probably built by Dr. John Cairns whose
home next door was very similar. Dr. Cairns, a Scot who had
spent many years in Hong Kong, designed each house after the
British colonial square bungalow with open verandahs on
all sides and a detached kitchen, seen on the right in the
photograph, which was taken in 1910. The grounds of both
houses were planted with exotic trees and shrubs from
the Orient. After Dr. Cairns' death in 1886, his house was
razed and a three-story Victorian delight was built on the
site by Australian wool merchant John Shoobert for his family.
Other than the glass-enclosed verandahs, the Tillinghast
house is little changed today and is architecturally unique
in Sausalito.

CHRISTIANSEN

Interior, Casa Madrona Hotel

37

*Old Town in 1882 (above) reflects little of the building boom going on in New Town. The fancy building with the flagpole is the home of the Pacific Yacht Club. Below it is Captain Leonard Story's home built in 1850. The government store houses, hotels, and sawmill of the Botts era are long gone. The imposing structure at the left in the photograph is the Saucelito Smelting Works, established in 1878.*

*Sausalito Boulevard high above Old Town c. 1890 (below) with Angel Island in the background. The new road was part of a plan to promote interest in lots in Old Town.*

*The Pines (above), built in 1888 was the residence of Major and Mrs. Orson C. Miller, and was situated appropriately on Miller Avenue.*

Meanwhile in Old Saucelito, or "Old Town" as it is now called, little had changed since Charles Botts' initial venture. The Pacific Yacht Club made its debut in 1878. A few homes had been built. A few saloons had come and gone, and Botts, who died in 1884, had long since sold his interests to John Turney and others. The new owners incorporated in 1870 as the Old Saucelito Land & Drydock Company, and hoped to compete with the Sausalito Land & Ferry Company in New Town. Perhaps as the name implies, they still had plans to establish a drydock facility in the cove as an industrial base to attract business. But business was slow. By the 1880s, Old Town, isolated from the railroad, lay dormant once again.

Then in 1885 two guests registered at the El Monte Hotel set about changing that. Major Orson C. Miller and his wife had moved from San Francisco to Sausalito, like so many others, with a plan in mind.

Miller found title to the moribund lands of the Old Saucelito Land & Drydock Company in the hands of the Savings and Loan Society in San Francisco where it had been for the past three years. Miller approached Horace Davis, president of the Savings and Loan Society and by September 1887 the two had consummated a deal. Miller picked up all the unsold land in Old Town for $25,000.

He immediately set to work, surveying new streets and extending old ones further up the hillsides. He set up an auction house at the corner of Richardson and West Street and published a new map of available lots under the new corporate name: The Sausalito Bay Land Company. Miller's new map of 1888 shows Sausalito Boule-

vard for the first time, a sweeping semicircle with panoramic views extending from New Town to the Pacific Yacht Club lands. Sausalito Boulevard, with gentle grades suitable for horse-drawn wagons, was the key in reviving interest in Old Town. Central Avenue was also graded as a link between unsold Old Town lots and the lands of the Sausalito Land & Ferry Company. The new roads made Old Town more accessible by land. Previously, the only passage was the rock-strewn rough beach called Water Street, which was indeed water at high tide.

A few years before O. C. Miller arrived in Sausalito, there was a brief flurry of excitement in Old Town when manganese was discovered in the hills west of town. The ore found in the rock outcroppings was rich enough to justify small-scale mining. Tunnels were dug near the springs between present-day Prospect Avenue and Sausalito Boulevard. Henry H. Eames, an opportunistic inventor, built an ore reduction plant at the foot of Main Street to process the manganese ore. By 1880 the yield was about fifty tons of black oxide annually, hardly enough to make Sausalito a mining center. By 1893 the mines were abandoned and the Saucelito Smelting Works demolished to make way for Joseph Lowder's Walhalla.

Long forgotten, the mine entrances were sealed with fill from highway construction in the 1950s. In October, 1982, the mines were inadvertently rediscovered during slide-damage repairs following the disastrous rains of January that year. The tunnel uncovered extended over 100 feet horizontally into the hill and was lined with decaying redwood timbers. It has since been sealed.

39

*The informality of the San Francisco Yacht Club in the 1880s is demonstrated by this early morning scene: a quick "skinny dip" before breakfast. One stalwart about to go off the board seems a bit reluctant. Perhaps he is trying to gauge just how low the tide really is. What appears to be the Spreckels yacht* Lurline *of the Pacific Yacht Club rides at anchor in the distance.*

$S$ausalito in the 1880s generated considerable interest among San Francisco's rich. Saturday or Sunday excursions to Wildwood Glen or Damon's Grove had long been popular with the bourgeoisie. But now it became fashionable to be included on the guest list for a weekend at Hollyoaks or Hazel Mount, Casa Madrona or Alta Mira, the villas of Sausalito's aristocracy. However decorous these weekends might be, there was always something deemed slightly racy about Sausalito that livened up newspaper accounts of parties.

San Francisco started off early in a curious relationship with Sausalito. The natural beauty of Sausalito, its pure water and sunny climate were obvious, but it was seen as somehow "foreign," or at least European, filled with British, Portuguese, and French people, a place where protocol and convention did not quite adhere to the rough-and-tumble but God-fearing standards of San Francisco. Perhaps it was jealousy over the imagined (and sometimes real) lurid goings-on in the romantic "pleasure suburb" across the bay.

The founders of the Sausalito Land & Ferry Company were, for the most part, conservative San Francisco businessmen who worked hard to overcome Sausalito's reputation as a place of slight impropriety, where, as the *San Francisco Chronicle* reported in 1889, "Undoubtedly there is a considerable amount of quiet deviltry carried on in the snug little cottages." In an article that year entitled "Saucy Sausalito, A Motley Colony of English and Portuguese," a *Chronicle* writer revealed the popular conception of Sausalito, and in the bargain something of his own repressed fantasies.

"A number of English-Americans have made their home in the place, and it needs but the merest glance at the throng on the landing pier of a Saturday afternoon to decide that the 'blarsted Britishers' have found in Sausalito something that reminds them of their own 'tight little island,' for they swagger about in a pretentious style that would be highly unpolitic, not to say risky, in a typical American city. The Portuguese and the English colonies at Sausalito get along quite well.... They are not prone to interfere with each other, or to inquire into their neighbor's affairs. A New England hamlet of the same size as Sausalito would be the scene of as much scandal and gossip as would furnish the local paper with half a dozen columns of spicy locals every week.

But the Sausalitans have so many glass houses around them that they do not encourage stone-throwing. They are told that well-bred people do not inquire how much champagne finds its way on board a certain yacht every week. The Sausalito gossip would never dream it worth-while to speak of little mistakes made with latch-keys by belated husbands returning from a club-meeting in the wee small hours, [or question] why a new Juanita or Phryne or Belladonna has taken up her quarters at one of the mansions on the hill."

"The demure-looking damsels who come across in pairs on Saturday evening by the 5 o'clock boat from San Francisco could tell some interesting anecdotes of champagne suppers and altogether unanticipated stranding of yachts on convenient mud flats just before midnight. It is perhaps for this reason that discreet parents are rather shy of trusting their daughters out on these evening yachting trips, for it curiously happens that

though provisions run short the champagne is sure to have been thought of as the retiring tide leaves the stranded yacht in the blue moonlight.

"The Sunday yachting parties are comparatively select affairs, and many promising matrimonial flirtations are inaugurated this way. Once a month or thereabouts a ball is given at the El Monte Hotel, and here again there is a great gathering of sighing swains, laughing belles, and weary chaperones, whose chief pleasure is supposed to consist in accumulating evidence that their own youth has forever flown away."

In an attempt at praise, the reporter continues: "The artist and the camera fiend are wont to count Sausalito as a happy hunting ground. Wildwood Glen, when not invaded by a hoodlum picnic party is an exceedingly romantic, albeit damp and rhumaticky spot." He goes on to describe the town jail as "a crazy cage which would not hold a healthy school boy in durance vile for half an hour. It might be used for drunkards, but, as a resident explained, the law of sobriety can be very liberally construed. Just as old Joey Miller said, he never considered a man drunk as long as he could hold on to the grass."

A "local" basks in the quietude outside Pete Fagan's saloon (below) c. 1887. The San Francisco Yacht Club building is in the background on an otherwise unobstructed waterfront. In this view of Water Street looking south from Princess Street, the Sausalito Land & Ferry Company office and the Pioneer Boathouse are out of sight to the left.

*Members of the Pacific Yacht Club pose on the fifty-foot long balcony of their clubhouse. Justly proud of the club's setting and the spacious grounds, a member gave this florid description of the annual "Opening Day" social event in May: "Then the early roses in the flower beds are in full bloom, and the heliotrope and mignonette add to the fragrance of the queen of flowers. The grass on the lawns is as fresh as early dew. The hills, under which the Club-house nestles, are all with verdure clad. The blue water of the bay, smooth as glass; just beyond the shoreline, a group of beautiful yachts, lying at anchor, all dressed in bunting of brightest colors, on the deck of each, groups of ladies and gentlemen, gaily chatting together and admiring the scene afloat and ashore. In every face there is the light of pleasure—in every voice there is the ring of mirth. To add to the charm, there is the delicate sound of music from the band, leading the merry dancers in the hall."*

*A lithograph by Pacific Yacht Club member Gideon Denny shows the clubhouse in 1884.*

*The interior of the Pacific Yacht Club main hall with tables set for a banquet, c. 1890.*

$S$ausalito is a town with a nautical birthright. Her very existence and survival depended on watercraft of all types and on the masters and crews who manned them. It is only natural that along with ferryboats and fishing, boatbuilding and shipping, Sausalito became the home of the first yacht club on the West Coast, indeed, the second yacht club in America.

As wealth from the gold country and the Comstock Lode made its way to San Francisco, the beneficiaries of those riches, the bankers and merchant princes of Montgomery Street, acquired yachts befitting their station in life. Yachting as a recreational activity became popular with the status-conscious in San Francisco. The bay was workplace for the masses and playground for the rich. The San Francisco Yacht Club was started by a small group of yachting enthusiasts. In the summer of 1868, boat owners Edwin Moody, Richard Ogden, John Eckley, and Horace Platt of the Sausalito Land & Ferry Company, had sailed up the bay to Suscol on Napa Creek with families and guests for a 4th of July outing. The event went so well that shortly afterward they formed a permanent club, incorporating in 1869 as the San Francisco Yacht Club,

with Platt as first Commodore. They built a small clubhouse near San Francisco's Mission Bay (now filled), where they kept their boats anchored. On July 4th, 1869, they held the first yacht regatta west of the Mississippi, a race from Mission Rock to Fort Point and back. Following the race, Horace Platt's steam yacht *Amelia* towed the boats and their tired crews to Sausalito for an evening clambake. Platt happily showed off his latest investment in Sausalito real estate.

Word of the club spread among the boat owners of San Francisco, and new members quickly signed on, swelling the ranks until the little clubhouse on Long Bridge in Mission Bay was plainly inadequate. With its complement of new members, the club reorganized in 1873 and appointed a site selection committee for a new clubhouse. The newer members, represented on the selection committee by J. Clem Uhler, recommended "New Saucelito," where the Sausalito Land & Ferry Company was eager to sell lots. It is more than coincidence that Uhler was also partner in the Sausalito Land & Ferry Company. The older members (and those with larger boats) opted for "Old Saucelito," the deep water, anchorage in the cove.

*The Hill is filling up, c. 1890. Looking up from the first San Francisco Yacht Club building in Sausalito, many of the prime view lots are already occupied. Magnificent Hollyoaks is on the skyline, center. The triplet little Victorians along Water Street at the far right, two of which survive today, are called Lolita, Lucretia, and Lurline. Across Water Street from the San Francisco Yacht Club, and partially hidden by it, is the Dexter House where boxing champion "Gentleman Jim" Corbett trained for several of his fights.*

Unable to reconcile the schism, the minority favoring the cove broke away and formed their own club, the Pacific Yacht Club. The main body built its clubhouse on Sausalito's Water Street in 1878, and Richard L. Ogden became first Commodore of the "New Saucelito" San Francisco Yacht Club. The Pacific Yacht Club purchased land in the cove from the Old Saucelito Land & Drydock Company and christened their new clubhouse also in 1878, with John L. Eckley as Commodore.

The differences between the two clubs had a direct bearing on their fate. The Pacific Yacht Club, a smaller, more conservative group with their large ocean-going yachts, maintained a policy of life membership. A new member, once approved by the socially prominent and wealthy members, paid dues only once—upon joining. Over the years as the members grew older and retired from racing, or simply died off, there was no "new blood" to keep the club going. In 1899 the club faded out of existence; the clubhouse and grounds were sold to Adolph and John Spreckels for use as a summer house. They built a large boathouse on the shore to winter their yacht *Lurline*. In the 1950s when a large apartment complex was built on the site, the old boathouse was towed to Marinship, where it remained for many years as a houseboat.

The San Francisco Yacht Club, by contrast, had a constant infusion of new members paying annual dues. Many members had smaller, less pretentious boats, and the social occasions were less formal than those of the Pacific Yacht Club. As Sausalito grew, the San Francisco Yacht Club became a source of pride for residents even if they were not members. The newspapers were filled with accounts of races and yachting events. Yacht racing captured the fancy of plain folk as did reading about the marriages and trips abroad of the social elite. Even during the momentous world events of 1915, the *Sausalito News* featured front-page stories about yachting.

*The schooner* Chispa *(top right) in a rare early action shot of yachting on the bay. Isidor Gutte, her owner and skipper, was Commodore of the San Francisco Yacht Club eleven times between 1883 and 1896.*

*Past officers of the San Francisco Yacht Club, c. 1890, pose on the clubhouse deck. Photographer and yachtsman William Letts Oliver is third from the left; Charles Henry Harrison is hatless at center; and Isidor Gutte is on the far right, his gaze fixed on a distant yacht. Behind them is the Buffalo Hotel, soon to become notorious as a gambling hall.*

45

*The catamaran* Duster *(above), c. 1895, skims along the waterfront near the San Francisco Yacht Club with an unidentified sloop to starboard. The ferryboat* Sausalito *is in the NPCRR slip.*

*Isidor Gutte (left) and his mascot aboard* Chispa *prepare to fire a brass signal gun to mark the start of Opening Day, June 1, 1888.*

Beginning in the 1870s, the steam schooner, well suited to the needs of rich club men who liked to entertain guests with all the comforts of life ashore, had gradually superseded in popularity the large, ocean-going schooner yacht. This left the field of ocean racing to the sail enthusiasts, and yacht clubs began to reflect an interest in sailing rather than luxuriating. Smaller boats that didn't require professional crews became more popular, and the San Francisco Yacht Club eventually accepted even unconventional craft such as catamarans.

The original clubhouse of the San Francisco Yacht Club was destroyed by fire on March 21, 1897. Lost with it were all the records, trophies, and paintings of the club. Saddened but not disheartened, the members subscribed for larger, new quarters to be built on the same site. The new clubhouse, which stands today, was opened with a gala dance on April 23, 1898. The new clubhouse became a Sausalito landmark for the yachting fraternity on San Francisco Bay, and the setting for countless memorable parties and celebrations over the next twenty-five years.

*Photographer Walter A. Scott captured the schooner* Chispa *in a good breeze* c. 1885. Chispa, *a Spanish word for spark, was designed and built by Matthew Turner for Isidor Gutte in 1879. Gutte came from Germany to San Francisco during the gold rush and became a successful and highly respected insurance broker. Under Gutte's helm* Chispa *won many races and was considered one of the fastest boats on the bay. After Gutte's death in 1908,* Chispa *was sold and was last seen in 1917 hauling freight off the Mexican coast.*

*Photographer William Oliver's graceful yawl* Emerald *glides away from the clubhouse with Belvedere in the background, c. 1890.*

Finally, it was the automobile, more than anything else, that precipitated the decision to move the San Francisco Yacht Club from Sausalito. By the early 1920s, the limited space around the clubhouse had become inadequate for parking the automobiles of members and guests. In addition, Water Street was becoming more noisy and dusty from the increasing traffic, though this was a nuisance the yachtsmen could endure. But in 1922 the demon automobile struck a blow that could not be tolerated. A new ferry landing was built just north of the clubhouse by the Golden Gate Ferry Company, in competition with the railroad ferries at the old terminal. The new ferries were designed to carry automobiles to handle the growing demand of through traffic to Marin County.

*The San Francisco Yacht Club at the turn of the century. William Randolph Hearst's former home, Sea Point, looms on the Hill above the clubhouse. The new Spreckels boathouse is the large building at water's edge in the background.*

*William Oliver photographed his crew aboard* Emerald *in September, 1889, on the Sacramento Delta. Exhibiting something less than their usual jolly mood are, left to right: George Starry, Charles Yale, William Lowden, Bob Bailey, Captain Robert Fletcher, and Edward Hamilton.*

The wake of the large auto ferries passing close to the yacht club anchorage played havoc with mooring lines and boats as well, popping hatches and cabinet doors and all but swamping the smaller boats. A committee was appointed in 1926 to find a more protected location. The following year the San Francisco Yacht Club moved to Belvedere after first attempting to lease a site in San Francisco. In the early thirties the Sausalito clubhouse was sold to private interests. The old yacht club building, occupied today by restaurants, stands as a reminder of Sausalito's golden age of yachting.

49

*In 1897 William Randolph Hearst came to the aid of the financially distressed Sausalito Chapter, Native Sons of the Golden West. The grateful members renamed the chapter Sea Point Parlor in honor of Hearst's old Sausalito residence. In 1908, charter member Hearst bought new band uniforms for the Sea Point Parlor Drum Corps, shown here c. 1910.*

William Randolph Hearst was born in San Francisco in 1863 and passed his childhood years there in the rarified atmosphere of the affluent. Why he became fascinated by Sausalito is not recorded; perhaps even he never knew. As a child he no doubt heard stories about the new town and possibly even met Charles Harrison or Maurice Dore, who knew his father. After a three-year stint at Harvard, when he was expelled for his incessant pranks, William worked for two years at the *New York World,* his father's newspaper. He returned to San Francisco in 1887 in complete control of the *San Francisco Examiner,* another of his father's newspapers. Before long he was dazzling the journalistic world with his transformation of the sickly *Examiner* into "The Monarch of the Dailies."

When the twenty-three-year-old William rented a house in Sausalito overlooking the yacht club, it caused little stir among the British colony. He was just another millionaire's son, not the first or the last to seek refuge in Sausalito. Tall and slender, Hearst was shy in manner but possessed a strong will. His mistress from Harvard days, Tessie Powers, was soon ensconced in his Sausalito bachelor house, much to the chagrin of his mother, Phoebe Apperson Hearst. Sausalito society remained aloof from Hearst and his San Francisco friends. He was not invited to join the yacht club, and Tessie was ignored on the streets. It was not so much that Hearst kept a mistress, but that he made no effort to conceal it and was outwardly indifferent to criticism.

But in any case, the energetic Hearst had little time for Sausalito's social protocol. He had become fascinated by photography and was determined to perfect the process of reproducing photographs in newspapers. He had begun to collect an assortment of the finest photographic equipment available and with his friend George Pancoast began to look for space in which to conduct experiments on the reproduction process. In 1887 Henry Cartans, a local distiller, built a magnificent home on a promontory near Hearst's rented house. Sea Point, as Cartans called it, appealed to Hearst, and he leased it with an option to buy. He had the entire second floor of Sea Point converted into a photographic studio, complete with darkroom. Tessie Powers was also installed in the new quarters. Through a family-owned firm, the Piedmont Land & Cattle Company, Hearst bought Sea Point and gradually all the other lots around it — in effect, isolating himself from his Sausalito neighbors.

Since early childhood, when he first saw the palaces and museums of Europe, Hearst had dreamed of possessing a luxurious "castle" filled with the finest art and sculpture in the world. It would become a lifelong obsession. In April, 1890, construction began just below Sea Point on what was to be Hearst's castle, the first of many attempts to give form to a vision. But for reasons not entirely clear, work was stopped with only a retaining wall on Water Street and the foundations of the gatehouse completed. (Today a modern house stands on the massive stone and concrete foundation.)

George Hearst, William's father, died in 1891, leaving his considerable fortune to his wife rather than young William. William no doubt was humiliated by this comment on his free-spending ways. He left for an extended tour of Europe and Egypt with Tessie Powers and his comrade in photography, George Pancoast. When he returned, he set his sights on some property on the Marin headlands. In 1892, Senator Fenton of California, close friend of the late George Hearst, introduced a bill in Congress to dispose of about twenty acres of Lime Point Military Reservation. When it was discovered that Hearst wanted to buy seven acres of the property, the bill was quickly dropped. In the meantime, Phoebe Hearst finally had heard enough about Tessie Powers and her hold over William. She "persuaded" Tessie to leave with the promise never to return. William was heartbroken, but obedient to his mother's wishes. His response to these domestic and public defeats was to move out of Sea Point.

In 1910 Hearst returned briefly to Sausalito. With a wife, two children, and a New York architect in tow, he announced plans for an elaborate $250,000 Spanish-style home on his Sausalito property. Again he was distracted, and nothing was built. Acacia trees and wild grass took over the untended acreage. And when Hearst had Sea Point demolished in 1922, Sausalito thought it had heard the last of him. But in the 1930s when the city's proposed zoning ordinance listed the Hearst property as residential, he stepped forward with plans for a luxury hotel on Bridgeway that would rise to the crest where Sea Point once had stood and for a cluster of apartments along Atwood Avenue. The City Council accommodated Hearst by extending the commercial zone along Bridgeway to North Street, but no project was forthcoming. By 1943, with five "castles" including San Simeon, William Randolph Hearst surrendered his dream of a Sausalito palace, and the Sunical Land & Packing Company, a Hearst enterprise, sold his promontory overlooking the bay.

In the days before George Eastman developed his Kodak camera, photography was an expensive hobby, a fact that mattered little to the likes of William Randolph Hearst. In addition to cost, it was time consuming and required considerable skill and determination. Many of the photographs in this book are due to the efforts of hobbyists and professionals who took their unwieldy glass-plate cameras out of the studio to capture the charm and beauty of Sausalito.

*This group, c. 1885, about to embark on the tug* Annie *called themselves the "Hypos" after the hypo solution used in the developing process. In gratitude for their visual record, their names are recorded here: left to right, T. F. Palachio, Captain Hart of the* Annie, *R. S. Hooker, George A. Newhall, and Mr. S. Wilson. Ironically, one of their number remained on the pier to take this photograph and his name is lost to posterity, but it was probably George Whitney Reed. The vessel in the background is the ferryboat* San Rafael.

51

*Eugenia Baraty Schrimpf, daughter of merchant and landowner Jean Baptiste Baraty in the fashion of a Sausalito "Hill" lady of the turn of the century.*

*Winsor Cottage on Harrison Avenue, one of the many new homes built in Sausalito in the 1880s, as it appeared in 1910. It was not uncommon for affluent San Franciscans to purchase several adjoining lots from the Sausalito Land & Ferry Company and build one house as a residence and one or two as rentals. Thomas and Charlotte Winsor built this house and also Cheddar Villa next door.*

CHRISTIANSEN

The Heights was the home of Henry C. Campbell and his family. Campbell was a San Francisco attorney, land developer, Sausalito Town Trustee, President of the Sausalito Bay Land Water Company, and director of the Tamalpais Land Company. The Heights, built around 1880 at the end of Sweetbriar Lane, was a mansion befitting a man of his station. After his wife's death he married Ella Avery Reed, widow of the first rector of Christ Church, Frederick Wilcox Reed. As a wedding gift he built her a new mansion on Bulkley Avenue today known as Laneside. The Heights was demolished between 1907 and 1910.

When mansions like The Heights were torn down, many of the pieces were recycled. Parts of early houses, churches, arks, and sailing ships are incorporated in many existing Sausalito homes. The entrance of this waterfront cottage is from the Hickman Mansion on Sunshine Avenue, demolished in 1928.

*Early residents enjoyed tranquil Wildwood Glen and other hidden glades in the Sausalito hills. Photo by Joseph A. Mooser, April 7, 1889.*

*Central Avenue, 1910. Trees in Sausalito have always been controversial. At first it was the lack of them that prompted widespread planting of oak, bay laurel, pine, and cypress trees. As the trees grew to maturity blocking cherished views, tree cutting became a volatile issue. Eucalyptus trees were introduced early in Sausalito's history and with their rapid growth and tendency to blow over in windstorms, they too soon became a problem.* Sausalito News, *November, 1910: "Dr. Mays cut down a large eucalyptus tree. He has increased his supply of firewood and benefitted his neighbors by its removal. Who's next? Why not you? There are too many high trees in Sausalito."*

Laneside, on Bulkley Avenue was originally the Campbell Mansion built in 1892 by Henry C. Campbell as a wedding gift for his wife, Ella. She was the daughter of Mr. and Mrs. Francis Avery, who at the time Laneside was being built were moving into their new mansion, the Nook, next door at the head of Princess Street. Ella's father, who was secretary for the Sausalito Land & Ferry Company, hired noted architect Willis Polk to design The Nook. It is thought that Polk also designed Laneside at the same time.

The portals of the Nook, all that survives today of Francis Avery's mansion.

By the 1930s both homes had been converted to apartment houses. A new owner of the Campbell Mansion renamed it Laneside after her late husband, newspaperman Gillette Lane. The Nook was demolished in 1961 to make way for an apartment complex, but Laneside survived. The building today is within the Sausalito Historic District.

*Steamer* Queen *in Richardson's Bay, c. 1895.*

*Two of the young Wosser ladies visiting a square-rigger in Richardson's Bay, c. 1895. Many Sausalito families had seafaring relatives whose occasional visits to the bay were happy events. Children in particular enjoyed exploring the tall ships and listening to stories of far away places. Box cameras were carried on board to record lasting mementos like this one.*

*Aboard the three-masted bark* Lamoriciere, c. *1902.*

*Aboard a visiting square-rigger in Richardson's Bay.*

Sausalito's British colony could pull out the stops for visting captains and relatives: champagne suppers at the yacht club, or in the comfortable villas, with musicales and impromptu theatricals. In return the captain and his wife invited select groups to their finely appointed shipboard cabins, where perhaps a taste of Merry Olde England would be offered.

Riding at anchor in Richardson's Bay among the grain ships is the coastwise liner *Queen, c.* 1895, above left. In the foreground is the Spreckels yacht *Lurline.* The *Queen* was built in Philadelphia and arrived in San Francisco Bay August 25, 1882, as the Pacific Steamship Company's *Queen of the Pacific.* For almost fifty years she was, for San Franciscans and Sausalitans, a popular means of visiting friends and relatives in Los Angeles, Portland, or Seattle. In her later years she also carried passengers to Honolulu. In 1935 she became the *Queen Maru* under Japanese ownership and made a final voyage across the Pacific to the shipbreakers of Yokohama.

*As the grain business on the West Coast declined,
other types of vessels appeared more regularly in
Richardson's Bay. Coastal schooners, salmon barks
and steamers, and trans-Pacific packets were all familiar
visitors. The brigantine* Galilee, *shown here, was built
in Benicia by Matthew Turner in 1891. She made regular
runs to Tahiti carrying passengers and general cargo.
On her maiden voyage she set two records: nineteen days
out and twenty-two-and-one-half days return. In 1907 the*
Galilee *was chartered by the Carnegie Institute to
study compass variations in the Pacific. In this photograph
with the tug* Sante Fe, *she is in Carquinez Strait still
carrying special navigational equipment on her deck.*
Galilee *ended her days beached in Sausalito, and her hull
lies rotting today in the mud off Napa Street.*

*Standing proudly astride a cargo hatch, this unidentified
captain typifies the tough, confident, and resourceful
seafarers of the late nineteenth century. Many of these
men made Sausalito their final anchorage, living out their
lives in retirement near the ships they loved.*

Throughout the latter nineteenth century and well into the twentieth, it was common for grain ships to lay over in Richardson's Bay. Since the captain's family often accompanied him on voyages, children were enrolled in Sausalito schools to continue their education. The fall term, 1905, found Harry Purdie (above right) on his father's ship *Buteshire,* a three-masted bark in Richardson's Bay, attending Miss Isabel Porter's classes at South School. The *Buteshire* sailed for Tacoma in 1906, bound for Australia's wool market. Young Harry said goodbye to his teacher and friends in Sausalito and continued his odyssey around the world.

*Living quarters, below, for Captain Purdie and his family on board the* Buteshire *were probably similar to those on the bark* Lynton, *shown here in 1900.*

*Isabel Porter, an accomplished photographer, snapped this shot of her pupil Harry Purdie on board the* Buteshire *in Richardson's Bay.*

Ship Buteshire
Tacoma
Jan 6, 1906

Dear Miss Porter
I thank you for the pretty New Year card you painted for me. Mother has got it framed and it looks so nice.
We will be loaded on the ninth and it will be the 20th before we have all our crew on board.
We are going to Free-Mantle, Western Australia it will take 80 to 100 days to get there.
We don't like this place. Your Old pupil
Harry Palmer Purdie

59

Old Town in 1900, a scene of incredible tranquility.
The German biergarten, Walhalla is already seven years old. The scattered
hillside homes hint at the real estate activities of the Sausalito Bay Land
Company. The houses on the ridgeline are part of New Town, being developed
by the Sausalito Land & Ferry Company.

August 30, 1896: A picnic group (above right),
from San Francisco enjoying Spreckels Beach
in Old Town near the defunct Pacific Yacht
Club. The young lady in front center is
Angelena Antoni, who eight years later will
marry the man on her right, Scipio Ratto.
They will settle in Old Town and become two
of Sausalito's best-known citizens.

Not all houses built in early Sausalito were
villas or mansions. This house (right) built on Main
Street c. 1892 by millwright Charles Griswold
is a fine example of carpenter gothic, and is
in scale with the small lots in Old Town.
The house today appears much the same as
in this 1910 photograph.

"VISITORS NOT ALLOWED TO SHOOT OR BUILD
FIRES ON THE GOVERNMENT RESERVATION"
This rough fence was the southern boundary between
Sausalito and Lime Point Military Reservation,
later Fort Baker. Shown here c. 1890, the fence and
the warning sign above Edwards Avenue did little to
discourage hikers.

On October 25, 1893, Joseph "Al" Lowder fulfilled his dream of opening a true biergarten in Sausalito like those of his native Germany. The Walhalla opened for business that day as the first saloon in Old Town since the days of Charles Botts. The year before Lowder had sold his Buffalo Hotel on Water Street and had begun construction of the Walhalla on the site of the old smelter. The Walhalla quickly became a favorite with the German community and famous for sponsoring picnics and beer fests in Wildwood Glen. This photo, taken in 1910, shows the Walhalla under the proprietorship of Henry Siems, who leased it for five years from Joseph Lowder.

The Siems house on Main Street, 1910, with Anna and Henry Siems on the landing. In the right background is the Griswold house shown on the previous page.

Castle by the Sea, on the left in the above 1910 photo, and Cottage by the Sea on the right. Built in 1902 by Peter Wellnitz, the twin-turreted Castle by the Sea still stands today at Bridgeway and Richardson Street, although the one-story saloon on the bay side has been removed. Below it is a rare photograph, c. 1905, of the interior of Castle by the Sea saloon in the heyday of Sausalito's gambling rooms.

Contrary to popular legend, there is no documentation that Jack London ever was a boarder at the Castle by the Sea. If he spent any time at all in Sausalito, it would more likely have been in the saloon or across the street at Dan Eustace's Cottage by the Sea, also a saloon. This watering hole was called the "Last Chance Saloon" by soldiers returning on foot to Fort Baker in the wee hours of morning.

*This group of East Bay amateur photographers who called themselves the "Merry Tramps" are posed at the Military Reservation fence c. 1887. The mansion on the ridge to the left is The Heights of Henry Campbell, and to the right, Henry Cartan's Sea Point, later the home of William Randolph Hearst.*

*Fort Baker Parade Ground c. 1907. This scene, showing the officers' quarters on the right and barracks on the left, is almost unchanged today, except for the Golden Gate Bridge.*

*The guardhouse at Fort Baker, c. 1905, with soldiers of the 68th Company of Coast Artillery. The Parade Ground, seeded with Australian Rye grass, also served as part of the Sausalito Golf Course. The links were kept mowed by 150 sheep, kept on reservation for that purpose. The* Sausalito Advocate *complained in 1902: "Those sheep that we expected to see develop such fine appetites that they would consume all the grass in which the balls are so effectively lost, we say are frauds. They seem to enjoy the fine views so much as the average Sausalitan, and may always be found nibbling on hill tops while the grass on the links grows apace. Can't the shepherd receive instructions to restrain their mountain climbing proclivities and keep them actually on the links?"*

Sausalito's closest and oldest neighbor is the United States Army. Ever since the southern portion of *Rancho del Sausalito* was sold to the federal government in 1866, the military has played a role in the town's development. The Lime Point Military Reservation (later Fort Baker) was part of a grand plan to defend the Golden Gate.

Shortly after California was seized from Mexico in 1846, it became apparent that a permanent military garrison was needed in San Francisco Bay. After all, a mere handful of Americans under Frémont had had no difficulty capturing the all-but-abandoned Presidio. The bay was defenseless against a determined aggressor. Other nations watched with keen interest as the United States attempted to hold the vast new territory with a thin thread of military occupation bravely called the "Tenth Military Department," assisted by the United States Naval Squadron on the Pacific Ocean.

The chaos resulting from the gold rush again demonstrated the glaring need for a strong military presence as hundreds of ships from many nations sailed through the Golden Gate. In the early 1850s a defense plan was mapped out, and Congress appropriated funds for the project. Key points around the bay would be taken or purchased,

and permanent artillery batteries installed. The U.S. Army occupied the Presidio in San Francisco and built new fortifications at the site of the old Mexican *castillo* at *Punta del Cantil Blanco* (white cliff point), which would be called Fort Winfield Scott (later to become Fort Point). At *Punta de San José* it built Fort Mason, named in 1882 for the second military governor of California, Col. Richard Barnes Mason. Alcatraz and Angel Island were also occupied by the military. Only the north shore of the Golden Gate remained unprotected.

The Army negotiated with William Richardson in 1854 for the Marin headlands, including *Punta de San Carlos,* now called Lime Point after the rocks' most obvious characteristic, a coating of bird guano. (The Americans were far less elegant in selecting place names than were the Spanish or Mexicans.) After Richardson turned over the affairs of *Rancho del Sausalito* to Samuel Throckmorton in 1855, Throckmorton offered 1,899 acres of Lime Point to the Army for $200,000. Congress felt that the price was exorbitant and initiated a period of negotiations and litigations with Throckmorton that lasted ten years. After the Civil War, during which not a shot was fired from Bay Area fortifications, Congress cooled on the idea of coastal fortifications. Throckmorton, sensing his opportunity might be slipping away, quickly reduced the asking price and in 1866 sold the entire headlands for $125,000 to the United States government.

Plans slowly got under way for construction of an artillery battery at Gravelly Beach (later Kirby Cove) on the newly acquired military reservation. Only two of the twelve planned gun emplacements were ever built, and in 1873 a single gun, a fifteen-inch smoothbore Rodman, was installed. For the next fifteen years, that gun and the rusty old fog signal canon at Point Bonita were the only protection for the north shore of the Golden Gate. In 1897 a permanent fort was established at Horseshoe Cove, east of Gravelly Beach, consisting of two wooden barracks towed on barges from the Presidio, and a guardhouse, corral, and stables—all built on site. Named in honor of Col. Edward Dickinson Baker, who was killed in the Civil War, the new post was manned by Battery I, 3rd Artillery, U.S. Army, transferred from Fort McDowell on Angel Island.

For the next ten years Fort Baker grew at a steady pace. Lessons learned by Admiral Dewey at Manila Bay in 1898 demonstrated the importance of modern coastal defenses. New shore batteries were installed and a road graded around Yellow Bluff to Sausalito, thereby making the fort accessible by land as well as by sea. The marshy beach was filled and seeded to become a parade ground; trees were planted, sewers and water mains laid; and brick barracks, a powerhouse, and splendid Victorian officers' quarters were built. Around 1900, the commandant of Fort Baker, an avid golfer, allowed a golf course to be added to the parade ground. Sausalito golfers designed the course and constructed all the traps and greens. It was so popular that the Sausalito Golf Club was organized and a clubhouse built near the edge of the parade ground.

*Revenue Cutter* Hugh McCulloch, *in 1908 from a glass-plate photograph by William Sutherland. The Revenue Cutter* Thetis *is outboard of the* McCulloch *as the ferryboat* Sausalito *fills the sky with coal smoke. A veteran of the Battle of Manila Bay in 1898, the* McCulloch *carried the news of Admiral Dewey's victory to Hong Kong, where it was flashed around the world. Stationed in San Francisco Bay after the Spanish-American War, she patroled from the Mexican border to the Oregon border until 1906, assisting vessels in distress and searching for derelicts and smugglers. Other cutters often anchored in Richardson's Bay were the* Alert, Bear, Thetis, *and* Albatross.
*The Revenue Service became the U.S. Coast Guard in 1915 and the* Hugh McCulloch *was transferred to the new service. In 1917 she was lost in a collision off Point Conception.*

*A military presence in Sausalito at the turn of the century were the revenue cutters anchored in the cove off Old Town. Seen from the deck of the Speckels House (formerly the Pacific Yacht Club), with its Civil War-vintage canons, Revenue Cutter* Hugh McCulloch *gets up a little steam, c. 1910.*

*Captain John Cassin Cantwell, left, commander of the Revenue Cutter* Hugh McCulloch *in 1905. In 1884 as a twenty-five-year-old Lieutenant aboard the Revenue Service steamer* Corwin, *Cantwell participated in explorations near the Kobuk River in Alaska, where a small settlement north of Anchorage still bears his name. He built his home, Sweetbriar, in Sausalito in 1903 and was a permanent resident thereafter. Captain Cantwell became well known for his civic involvement and stem-winding speeches at town hall meetings.*

*Marine artist William Alexander Coulter, his wife Harriet, and their children Stuart, James, and Helen, and dog Moro at their home on Fourth Street in Sausalito. In the 1890s Coulter worked for the* San Francisco Call *making pen and ink sketches of maritime news events— shipwrecks, arrivals of vessels in the Golden Gate, and sea battles of the Spanish-American War. Descriptions of battles were telegraphed to him, and he used his imagination to fill in missing details.*

The military reservation had long been a favorite with Sausalito hikers. Picnics on grassy hills overlooking San Francisco and outings to the fog signal at Point Bonita were easy one-day jaunts from town. Now the permanently manned fort became a neighboring "town" for Sausalito. Children of officers stationed at the fort attended Sausalito schools. Local merchants traded regularly with the men and officers and their families. Dances and parties at the post were well attended by Sausalitans, and weekend baseball games and basketball games became regular events. In spite of an official gate at the Sausalito entrance to Fort Baker, civilians were welcome on the grounds, and the relationship between the two "towns" was cordial.

Formation of a new branch of the Army, the Coast Artillery Corps, in 1907 signaled a change in military-civilian relations that affected Sausalito and Fort Baker. Increasing militarism in Europe had prompted Germany and Britain to expand their navies with modern battleships, dreadnoughts capable of shelling coastal cities from miles at sea. The coast lines of the United States became more vulnerable than ever before. President Theodore Roosevelt sent a U.S. Navy fleet on a round-the-world cruise to show the flag in foreign ports and demonstrate that the United States was a substantial sea power. International sabre-rattling and rumors of potential sabotage closed the open door policy of coastal military posts. Sausalito's golf course at Fort Baker was

closed; dances, picnics, and social events were curtailed; and cameras were banned. New, more powerful guns were installed, and an air of secrecy pervaded the fort. In 1908 when the fleet reached San Francisco Bay, visitors, who came by the thousands, were permitted to view the fleet's arrival from the Marin headlands, but were instructed to confine themselves to specific pathways and to avoid gun emplacements and other "sensitive" areas. In spite of increased security measures, relations between Fort Baker and Sausalito remained friendly.

Over the years the coastal shore batteries became obsolete, and except for brief periods during World War I and World War II, the headlands forts have seen diminishing activity. The old Lime Point Military Reservation became part of the Golden Gate National Recreation Area in 1972. Fort Baker, last of the active forts on the Golden Gate's north shore, will be phased out to become part of the National Park system.

Military presence in the Marin headlands has always been low-key. Construction has been confined mainly to roads, underground bunkers, and gun emplacements, leaving all of the rolling hills and rocky coastline in a natural state. Inadvertently, the U.S. Army has helped create a setting for Sausalito that is unique. The lands to the south and west of Sausalito are very much as they were 150 years ago. William Richardson today would have no difficulty in recognizing this part of his *Rancho del Sausalito.*

*The United States Battle Fleet visits San Francisco Bay. After completing the first leg of an
around the world cruise, from New York around Cape Horn to California, the long-anticipated entry
through the Golden Gate came off as scheduled. On May 6, 1908, sixteen battleships and their escorts, totaling
forty-two vessels steamed in a single file presenting a spectacular display to the throngs crowded along
the cliffs above Fort Baker and Point Bonita. During their two-week respite before setting out across
Pacific, the ships anchored off Yerba Buena Island.*

*Standing on the bridge of the Battleship*
New Jersey, *Walter A. Scott took this photo on
May 16, 1908, as civilian visitors mingled
with the sailors on deck. Directly astern is the*
New Jersey's *sister ship,* U.S.S. Georgia, *also
receiving visitors. Thousands of northern
Californians passed through Sausalito and under
the welcome arch on El Portal on their way to
view the fleet. The decorated arch gave Sausalitans a sense of participation in the event.*
*(See page 81.)*

Photographer William Sutherland with his glass-plate camera captured the Lady Ada hauled out next to the Walhalla at the foot of Main Street in 1908 (top left). Built in 1904 by W. F. Stone Shipyard in San Francisco, the fifty-nine-foot schooner was owned by Isidore Zellerbach and has had a long career on the bay.

Captain Isidor Gutte (third from left), and friends, taking a breather on Chispa, c. 1895.

San Francisco Yacht Club(left), in 1902, taken from the same angle as the photo of the old yacht club building on page 44.

Hauling the main sheet, c. 1895 on Emerald.

*Mathias Lange, c. 1900.*

Mathias Lange went to sea as a boy from Norway and arrived in San Francisco in the 1880s. By 1904 he was well established as a boatman on the bay, with a small fleet of work boats. He was also custodian and steward for the San Francisco Yacht Club and in 1907 occupied a little building just north of the clubhouse. For the next thirty years he operated as Lange's Launch Company from there, becoming a well-known fixture on the waterfront. His gasoline-powered launches did yeoman service over the years, towing stranded sailboats, carrying fishing parties, delivering late commuters to San Francisco and newspapers to Mile Rock lighthouse. Matt Lange, or as he was called in later years, Pop Lange, was a tireless worker who branched out into the bait business; he sold fresh crab, made sandwiches for party cruises, and carried visitors to ships at anchor.

Remarkably, Matt Lange's building survives today. In 1926 it was moved closer to the yacht club building to make room for the Golden Gate Ferry Company landing. It has been a bar, a restaurant, and has been pushed out, added to, remodeled, and redecorated. But underneath, it is still the same building.

*From the* Sausalito News, *January, 1910: "Hunters Attention! Sloop* Fulton *at your service for a good duck hunt on the bay shore. Fine commodious cabin accommodations. A launch to tow her to and from anchorage."*
*Southern Marin was once a hunter's paradise: shooting geese in Richardson's Bay from the yacht* Idler, c. *1890.*

*One of Matt Lange's boats,* Marie L, *with Lange at the helm and a picnic-bound party on board. Taken from Lange's Launch building,* c. *1912.*

*BEFORE: July 4, 1893   Looking north along Water Street from the NPCRR ferry wharf, the Casa Madrona is nestled in the trees above the three-story Tamalpais Hotel and a row of wooden store fronts. Hunter's Resort is just out of the picture to the left.*

*AFTER: July 5, 1893  Stunned residents and shopkeepers pick through the rubble of Sausalito's downtown business district on the morning after. The Casa Madrona, untouched by the fire, is obscured by smoke. The rest, including Hunter's Resort, is ashes.*

*"While the Tamalpais Hotel building was being consumed the boiler in the basement exploded, sending the roof 300 feet in the air. No one was hurt. The explosion was heard for miles around."*
—S.F. Examiner, *July 5, 1893*

Hunter's Resort on Water Street (lower left) as it appeared on the fateful day of July 4th, 1893. This wood frame building stood where the old Sausalito City Hall is today across from *Plaza Viña del Mar.* Its lofty title suggests a retreat for weary sportsmen returning from the hunt. In reality it was just another Sausalito saloon. The local denizens of Hunter's Resort dragged their chairs onto the porch that Fourth of July evening, to watch the fireworks launched from the El Monte Hotel on the hillside above. Unnoticed, a sputtering skyrocket or firecracker landed on the roof of Hunter's Resort setting it ablaze. By the time the fire was noticed it was out of control, and the fireworks display became a thing to behold.

Although no one was injured, ten buildings were destroyed, almost the entire business district of Sausalito.

*I*n the 1880s, with telegraph lines strung across America and telephone service in most cities, a new form of gambling emerged. Results of horse races could be relayed to almost anywhere there was a telegraph key. At Eastern tracks a wire service was established to flash results to subscribing "poolrooms," literally "rooms where betting pools were organized." In California this meant that one could spend the entire day in a poolroom as race results came in from New York, then Chicago, and finally the West Coast. Most cities in California soon outlawed off-track poolrooms because they were completely unregulated. They were also, invariably, saloons. The poolrooms, it was claimed, drained the vigor from American manhood (and the dollars, as well) and were hangouts for loafers, criminal types, and drunks. In an effort to clean up the notorious Barbary Coast, San Francisco outlawed poolroom betting around 1894; the ordinance only drove the poolrooms underground and created a new criminal profession of "bookie." A few poolroom operators, preferring to stay legal, looked elsewhere for a town where they might be welcome.

As part of incorporation proceedings in 1893, the Sausalito Board of Trustees had outlawed poolrooms and gambling in general. Displaced poolroom operators urged the board to reconsider. Properly licensed poolrooms, they argued, could be a great revenue source for the town and would draw people from San Francisco to Sausalito, where they would perhaps become permanent residents. Sausalito had a tradition of decent waterfront saloons that had never been particularly troublesome. Alcohol had always been served in hotels and cafes as a matter of course. So the addition of legalized gambling on the "Sport of Kings" seemed a logical extension of gentlemanly activity for Sausalito. The Board of Trustees was persuaded to allow licensed poolrooms in Sausalito, whose residents reacted in mixed fashion to the news. A San Rafael paper commented in 1894: "The poolroom business which has been driven out of the sinful metropolis [San Francisco] as too vile to be tolerated there and forbidden to locate in classic Oakland, has established quarters and opened transactions in Sausalito. We feel they will be ejected from Sausalito as public sentiment finds expression. It is a wonder they are allowed to open."

A prosperous and well-liked gambler from Sacramento, Frank Daroux, opened Sausalito's first poolroom in the Barreiros Building on Water Street (749 Bridgeway). A politician by nature, Daroux soon became active in local affairs, assisting in the election of Adolph Sylva, a wealthy member of Sausalito's English colony, to the Board of Trustees. Around 1900, Daroux and Company moved their poolroom operation to the Buffalo Hotel, built on pilings over the water near the foot of Princess Street. The Barreiros Building soon housed a second licensed poolroom, run by Joe Harvey and Company. Opposition to poolroom gambling quickly organized as the Municipal Improvement Club, dedicated to ridding Sausalito of the menace. Members' worst fears were realized as ferryboats began arriving filled with "undesirables" from San Francisco. The local saloons that had been friendly, rather quiet places, became scenes of countless brawls, drunken arguments, and raucous celebrations. Water Street on race days was a crowded, hostile place lined with saloons out of which drunks stumbled, leering and shouting obscenities at passers-by. "A decent woman didn't like to pass through Water Street to get to the ferry. The whole town smelled of stale beer," recalled Rebecca Chambers in her memoirs of early Sausalito.

---

*"We call on the citizens of Sausalito to rise in their might and remove this great evil from their midst . . ."*
— *The* Sausalito Advocate

---

Attorney Archibald Treat, president of the Improvement Club, circulated a petition calling for elimination of the poolrooms, but it was ignored by the progambling majority of the Board of Trustees. The *Sausalito News,* dedicated to boosterism and disinclined to print anything negative about Sausalito, remained silent on the issue. The Improvement Club countered in September, 1900, with its own newspaper, the *Sausalito Advocate,* with Edward Sparrow, editor and a board including O. C. Miller, George Harlan, and P. J. Elliott among others, Here was the means to take on the "poolies" and challenge the "push," a collective term for the paid poolroom advocates that always showed up at town meetings. Battle lines were drawn. Hill dwellers and the Portuguese community were overwhelmingly against the gamblers. Although Water Street merchants like Charlie Becker, Fred Fiedler, Scipio Ratto, and John Mecchi had close friends among the saloon owners, they also opposed the poolrooms. The railroad, profiting by increased ferry patronage, remained silent. The "anti-poolies" succeeded in placing the issue before the voters in 1901. When the measure to ban the poolrooms failed, the Improvement Club accused the opposition of vote tampering and fraud,

*A group of impressively dressed "anti-poolies," including Fred Fiedler, stand in front of Fiedler's Store on Water Street (670 Bridgeway) in 1910. They typify the civic-minded merchants and residents who were determined to rid Sausalito of saloon riffraff. This building still stands today although a second story was added in 1981.*

while the gamblers piously claimed the vote showed public support for the poolrooms.

But what had happened was legal, if not ethical. Most California towns of the period had loose residency requirements for voting in municipal elections. Anyone who had lived in Sausalito for two weeks or more could vote. So the poolroom operators had simply rounded up men in San Francisco who could be easily bribed and boarded them at the Buffalo Hotel in Sausalito for the two weeks prior to the election. The Improvement Club's next tack was to get a bill outlawing poolrooms introduced in the California Legislature. But Archie Treat returned to town with the sad news that a committee had rejected the bill, advising Sausalito to clean up its own mess, since it was strictly a local issue. Treat vowed to continue the fight to "improve Sausalito and get it from the rut of rottenness that it now flounders in."

The next target was the Sausalito Board of Trustees who were facing an election in April, 1902. Three members, two of them "poolies," were up for reelection. The Improvement Club ran two well-respected candidates,

James Jones and William Grant Morrow, board member of the *Advocate*. Gambler Joe Harvey had had a falling out with Mayor Sylva allegedly over Sylva's cut of poolroom profits. Resulting litigation split the allegiance of the "poolies" and buoyed the hopes of the "anti-poolies." A Marin County Grand Jury report, the icing on the cake, was widely circulated in January, 1902. It read, in part: "The Grand Jury has investigated at considerable length the condition of affairs in the town of Sausalito, and wishes to condemn in the severest manner the political situation of that city. Since the poolroom gamblers have gained a foothold in Sausalito, the people of Marin county are continually hearing of frauds at elections, of money being used directly and indirectly to secure the gamblers in power and of many demoralizing intrigues that follow in the train of this illegitimate public gambling.

"We consider it against good public policy that these open public gambling houses are allowed to exist. Particularly it is a public disgrace when a community appears to elect their town officials on a distinctly pro-poolroom ticket.

"We have examined the Trustees of Sausalito and find that three were directly elected by the poolrooms; that at the present time two of them consider that they represent the poolrooms and not the citizens of Sausalito. These two public officials declare under oath that they believe this business, which is considered all over the state as illegitimate and which is driven from every community, is for the best interests of Sausalito.

"We call on the citizens of Sausalito to rise in their might and remove this great evil from their midst and the disgrace from the community."

Confident of victory, the antigambling forces were stunned by the defeat of Jones and Morrow at the polls. The *Advocate* lashed out at the turn of events. "A seemingly popular decision at the polls in favor of public gaming houses does not make a business legitimate. We all know the force of money in a small community and we all know how that money was used last April. As long as there is one spark of American manhood left in Sausalito, just so long will any demoralizing influences be fought. The Municipal Improvement Club is here to stay and will fight the gamblers at every turn."

Actually the election was a victory for the "antipoolies," because Adolph Sylva had been defeated and a moderate, E. H. Shoemaker, elected in his place. Also a staunch opponent of gambling, town barber Jacques Thomas was reelected and named mayor.

The new Board of Trustees declared the poolrooms to be public nuisances and brought suit against Harvey and Daroux, and against M. T. Barreiros and Charles Forest, the owners of the property where the two poolrooms were located. After a lengthy trial, the gamblers won again when a San Francisco Superior Court judge decided that the poolrooms did not violate Sausalito's nuisance ordinance.

Unable to rid the town of poolrooms, the Board of Trustees went after the saloons, raising the annual fee for saloon licenses and refusing to issue any new permits. Through the town marshall they also cracked down on public drunkenness and disturbing the peace. Frank Daroux, now called the "Gambler King," moved to San Francisco around 1906 where he became a political power broker, but he kept an interest in the Buffalo Hotel poolroom. Reformers continued to push for elimination of legalized gambling, and in 1909 the California Legislature outlawed off-track betting. The Sausalito poolrooms closed their doors. By that time most of the disreputable saloons were long gone, replaced by respectable family restaurants like the Arbordale. And the Board of Trustees was dominated by men who put civic pride and service above personal gain.

Scipio Ratto in many ways exemplified the Sausalito reformers who took the town out of the hands of the gambling interests and gave it back to the residents, and who

*John Mecchi stands in front of his store on Water Street in 1910. In the doorway wearing a grocer's apron is his partner, Scipio Ratto. On the left is Manuel Machado, city worker, fireman and one-time dog catcher. The Ferry Cafe at that time was one of the many Sausalito saloons. Both buildings exist today across from Plaza Viña del Mar.*

*Scipio Ratto, on the left in the photo above, taken at Dawson City during the Alaskan gold rush in 1899. Note the dog team in use even during the summer.*

worked tirelessly over the years to improve life in their town. Ratto was born in San Francisco in 1869, son of a Mother Lode general store proprietor who came to California from Italy in 1852. Scipio's father ran two San Francisco bakeries and what few days off the family had were spent in Sausalito. It was on these picnic outings that Scipio fell in love not only with Sausalito but also with Angelena Antoni, whose parents had come over land to California during the Gold Rush.

When gold was discovered in the Yukon, Scipio Ratto set out for the Klondike. He arrived in Juneau in the summer of 1897, full of high hopes and big plans. He went up the Whitehorse River in search of gold. After almost a year of struggling with freezing cold, scurvy, wild rivers, lots of ice, and very little gold, Ratto made his way to Dawson City, then a scruffy boom town crowded with miners and merchants. He eventually found work in George Biber's general store in 1899. Like most others, he left the Yukon no richer than when he arrived.

In 1904 at age thirty-five, Scipio Ratto was ready to settle down. He married his sweetheart Angelena and moved to Sausalito, where he formed a partnership with John Mecchi in 1905. Ratto maintained a successful business in Sausalito until he retired in 1935.

Downtown Sausalito resembled the rough and tumble mining camps of the Yukon when Ratto arrived. The streets were mud holes, rowdy drunks were common on Water Street, and the gambling rooms and saloons seemed like the principal business. Ratto and his wife became political activists, taking part in almost every effort to improve their town as well as rearing two daughters. He helped form the Old Town Social Club and was an officer in the South Sausalito Improvement Club, and served as Assistant Chief of the Sausalito Volunteer Fire Department in 1912. He was a charter member of the Sausalito Lions Club and the Chamber of Commerce, and a member of the Native Sons of the Golden West for over forty years. In his spare time he served on the Sausalito School Board, from 1922 to 1940, and was a member of both the Eagles and the Elks Club.

*After 1902 saloon licenses were hard to come by in Sausalito. This one, issued in 1905 to Manuel Ignacio, is good for only three months.*

*Before: The Pond seen from the railroad wharf c. 1902. Claudiano's Yacht House is on the far right, Arbordale on the left. The dingy El Monte Hotel has taken the name but not the class of its famous predecessor. The* Sausalito Advocate *in 1900 said: "It is a very pretty sight to witness some of the rigs driven by fair daughters, waiting for expected guests. How much would be added to the scene if that big water hole was converted to a park."*

*After: The Pond (right) is now a pleasant plaza. The occasion is Admission Day, September 9, 1909, as the queen's float passes by the welcome arch on El Portal, a leftover from the 1908 visit of the Great White Fleet to San Francisco Bay. The new Presbyterian church is on the Hill above the hotel now called The Ferry Cafe.*

The "Pond" was the symbol of all that was rotten in Sausalito. Cut off from tidal action by the maze of pilings supporting the railroad wharf, it was a stagnant backwash, a repository of garbage, sewage, and the flotsam and jetsam of saloon-lined Water Street. Vile vapors rising from its surface were blamed for everything from bad tempers to cholera. At low tide huge wharf rats scurried over slime-covered rocks and rotted pilings along its edges and under dilapidated Claudiano's Yacht House, a hotel and restaurant perched on stilts over the Pond. Residents complained about the stench they endured while waiting for ferryboats and trains. Commuters preferred not to think about it as they hurried on their way.

The financially strained North Pacific Coast Railroad, which had created the Pond by expanding the wharf, ignored the problem and complaints from the Sausalito Board of Trustees. But Jacques Thomas, chosen mayor in 1902 following his reelection to the Trustees, made elimination of the Pond a personal goal. He took literally his election pledge to clean up Sausalito. When in that same year the North Shore Railroad took over from the ailing North Pacific Coast, Thomas was quick to approach the new management. The North Shore announced plans to improve and modernize the entire line: new electric commuter trains, new track with fewer curves, and a new Sausalito wharf and train terminal. Thomas persuaded the company to include a landscaped plaza in front of the new terminal building as part of the improvements. The *Sausalito News* happily reported the decision: "The eternal source of trouble, bickering and un-noseable odors—the Pond—will be filled, [and] the rickety building along its front [Peter Claudiano's Yacht House] will be removed."

The new plaza was named Depot Park, but for most grateful citizens it was known as Thomas's Park for many years. After Jacques Thomas's untimely death in 1912, a memorial drinking fountain was set in the low stone wall surrounding the plaza, with the following simple inscription: Dedicated to Jacques Thomas, Founder of this Park, Sept. 1912.

*Water Street in 1904 with the new plaza, a ship's mast serving as a flagpole. The Bank of Sausalito building, far right, will serve as the Sausalito City Hall from 1925 to 1974.*

*The Arbordale, c. 1905, after a street and plaza were created by filling the Pond.*

*Alvina Kistenmacher and her daughter Elaine on the boardwalk between the saloon and dining room at the Arbordale, c. 1905.*

The wooden structure that was to become the Arbordale was built on the bay side of Water Street as close as possible to the railroad and ferry wharf. As far back as anyone could remember, there had been a saloon in the building, which probably dated back to 1875 when the wharf was built. At the turn of the century, it was a typical waterfront dive of the period called Nickles' Oyster Grotto. Then in 1902 Fred and Henry Kistenmacher, brothers from Germany, bought out Nickles and succeeded in transferring his saloon license too, a difficult feat under the anti-saloon Board of Trustees. But they had plans for the old place. They remodeled extensively, adding landscaping and grape arbors and large windows opening onto the bay. In the summer of 1902 Fred and his wife Alvina opened for business in the Arbordale, "the finest eating house on the bay." In addition to the saloon, now converted to a German beer garden and a

*The Kistenmachers in the Arbordale dining room, c. 1905.*
*The North Shore Railroad ferry slip is visible through the windows.*

"German Wine Room," the Arbordale featured an open cafe and a seafood dining room. Mrs. Kistenmacher, a former German opera singer, ran the kitchen while Fred kept the fine imported beer flowing and the good times rolling.

The railroad filled in the notorious and odoriferous "pond" next to the Arbordale in 1903, creating a landscaped town plaza and a new street frontage for the Arbordale. Over the years the industrious Kistenmachers improved the Arbordale, adding shrubs along El Portal, the new street next to the plaza, and enhancing the menu to attract ferryboat passengers. Twenty waiters served over 1,000 patrons a week at the Arbordale's peak of popularity around 1910. Tips were so generous that each waiter actually paid the Kistenmachers $10 a day for the privilege of waiting on tables. Mrs. Kistenmacher worked prodigiously, preparing a 35¢ seafood "merchant's lunch"

in the mornings and joyfully serving saloon customers until late hours, singing arias and bustling among the tables, often carrying up to six schooners of beer in each hand.

By 1915 the Arbordale's days of glory were over. Fred Kistenmacher had died, leaving a disheartened Alvina to carry on the business. Time had caught up with the ancient patched buildings, and the piers under the bayfront dining room sagged noticeably. New buildings were replacing the old ramshackle waterfront saloons. Henry Krause purchased the Arbordale and proposed a two-story hotel "with all modern conveniences" for the site. In August, 1915, the Dolan Wrecking Company pulled down the Arbordale, one of the last relics of Sausalito's poolroom era. The hotel with its Mission-style stucco facade, restaurant, and dance hall soon became a popular Sausalito gathering place, but the Arbordale lived on as a pleasant memory.

*Sausalito children on a clear afternoon in 1901 overlooking Central School at center. Opened for classes in 1888, Central School was moved down the hill to the corner of Caledonia and Litho Streets in 1926 where it remains today. A new Central School was built on the original site on Litho Street between Caledonia and Bonita Streets, and it became the Sausalito City Hall and library in 1975.*

*New Town, c. 1909, with Saint Mary, Star of the Sea Church in the center, and the bell tower of Central School visible at lower left.*

By the time the poolrooms were closed down and Water Street was tamed after the turn of the century, Sausalito had reached a kind of municipal maturity. The town's population had doubled in twenty years, reaching 2,380 by 1910, with scores of school-age children. A new school was built in Old Town in 1905 to handle the increased numbers. Service and improvement clubs sprang up. The civic improvements promised during debate on incorporation back in 1893 had not all materialized, but progress had been made. Most residents were active in their pursuit of municipal betterment.

*Sausalito's first school was in Old Town. This modest schoolhouse was built in 1869 on West Street and is today, with considerable modification, a private residence. A second school, named for William Richardson, was opened on Hannon's Hill in New Town in 1871, and it too is a private residence today.*

South School (above), built in 1905 between Third and Fourth Streets, was well liked by several generations of school children. Unlike most of Sausalito's public buildings, it has not survived. After being closed a few years before, it was demolished in 1958. Today the site is a public playground and tennis courts.

Central School 1911 (above right)
Miss Rose Obermilller's class has been making Japanese lanterns. A partial list of students: Margaret Ammerman, Elpha and Francis Baptiste, Walter Dreschsler, Elizabeth Elliott, Elsie Le Mar, Leonard Phelps, Fred and "Matz" Perry, Ernest Simas, Blanche Parsley, Frank and Amy Taylor, and Alpha Soares.

The Avilla residence (right), built in 1894, on Girard Avenue at Locust Road near the first Catholic church. The Sisters of Mercy from St. Gertrude's Academy in Rio Vista opened a convent and school there in 1910 as St. Mary's Academy. In 1911 the school, for grades two through eight, became Mount Carmel Academy, which lasted until 1940. The building no longer exists.

Central School became the Sausalito City Hall in 1975, but as this 1983 photograph shows, Sausalitans are not always quick to change things.

*The oldest grocery on Caledonia Street (if not in all of Sausalito), Broderick and Wright, owned this wagon and matched team. Taken in front of the store, out of view to the left, around 1912. Across the street is the home of Mayor and Mrs. Fred D. Linsley, which still stands at Turney and Caledonia Streets.*

*New Town looking north* c. 1904. *The old name of Turney Valley had dropped out of common usage by this time. William Richardson's old adobe is still visible in the center with a wooden second story added. Compare with the same view taken* c. 1880 *on page 20.*

*New Method Laundry wagon,* c. 1910. *Just as William Richardson had taken advantage of the pure water flowing from Wildwood Glen, so did Pierce John Elliott sixty years later. In 1902 he built the New Method Laundry on Caledonia Street near Pine Street. The name referred to a three-step method of disinfecting and washing. The business was carried on by his sons until 1977, when the laundry was sold and demolished.*

*About to embark on some summertime adventure (left), from the foot of Napa Street around 1915, these kids look like they're secretly hoping the photographer will topple backwards into the bay, camera and all.*

*Members of the Ritchie family in Wildwood Glen, c. 1912. The Glen holds fond memories for generations of Sausalitans. The Sausalito Land & Ferry Company built a large reservoir there that became a favorite swimming hole and fishing pond. Abandoned as a water source around 1914, the reservoir was drained in 1926 following the accidental drowning of two boys. The Glen also had a large wooden dance platform and briefly even a small hotel in the 1890s.*

*First picnic given by the Old Town Social Club in Wildwood Glen, July 3, 1910.*
*Mostly anonymous faces now, but at the time these people were the movers and shakers of Old Town.*

One of Sausalito's several amateur baseball teams, c. 1918.
Left to right, front row: Jack Lunt, Ed Baptiste, Tony Simas,
Terry McGowan, Frank Baptiste, Tom Bisagno,
Leo Quadros. Back row: Elmer Zaro, "Chick" Garcia,
Lee Pieraccini. Down in front: John Terris. The teams, with
names like The Alerts, The Sausalitos, The Red Bluffs, The Pets,
and The Heavy Weights, played at Fort Baker against teams
from Mill Valley, San Rafael, Fort Baker, and Alameda.

SAUSALITOS DEFEAT THE MILL VALLEYS,
*Sausalito News,* 1908." There was an unusually interesting baseball game between the Sausalitos and the Mill
Valleys last Sunday. The Sausalitos claim they won by
thirteen to eleven while the Mill Valleys claim honors
were even. The Sausalitos claim they were handicapped
by the absence of Ducksie McDevitt who overslept.
Brooks, their centerfielder, forgot his basket [glove] and
missed several good ones. Joe Pedro, while dreaming of
wedded bliss in leftfield, was brought out of his trance
by a sky ball striking him. The Mill Valley boys claim
they are onto [pitcher] Johnson's twirling and there will
be nothing to the return game."

September 7, 1907. Ready for a dip in Richardson's Bay are,
left to right: Theresa Antoni, May Peterzon, Angelena Antoni
Ratto (Mrs. S. G. Ratto).

The northern city limit of Sausalito was Nevada Street from 1893 to 1948. At the turn of the century, the hills north of Nevada Street still looked very much like they did in William Richardson's era. The area was used primarily as a pasturage for horses and cattle with a few small truck farms near Olima Street. Rodeo Avenue, shown here looking north, led to dairy farms west of Sausalito and to Sunnyhills Cemetery on the ridge above town. The horses are grazing on what is now Cypress Ridge, purchased by Sausalito citizens in 1976 as permanent open space.

This fine house on Tomales Street behind the distillery was built by twenty-three-year-old Frank Silva in 1910 for himself and his new bride. A skilled carpenter, Silva treated the house as a labor of love, adding handcarved moldings, delicate trim, and other finely crafted details. The house today is surrounded by trees and other houses, but it still stands out as a tribute to his skill.

*July, 1910. Frank J. Silva and his seventeen-year-old bride,*
*Mary Cardoza Silva on their wedding day.*

*Around the turn of the century, membership in social and fraternal organizations was a popular way of making acquaintances. The Foresters of America, Native Sons (and Daughters) of the Golden West, the Society of Old Friends, and ethnic groups like the British Benevolent Society and the German-American Society all flourished in Sausalito.*

The Sausalito Fire Department can trace its roots to February 6, 1888, when twenty-five prominent residents including J. W. Harrison, D. F. Tillinghast, John Broderick, William Reade, and Col. John Slinkey met at Arthur Jewett's blacksmith shop at Caledonia Street. At that meeting it was determined that a permanent volunteer fire department with modern equipment was a community necessity, and wheels were set in motion to accomplish that end.

Prior to that date fire protection was largely a matter of personal ability. Those with sufficient means built large water storage tanks next to their homes and kept fire hoses for personal use. Those less fortunate had to rely on bucket brigades or whatever means at hand, including a hasty exit if necessary. The North Pacific Coast Railroad maintained a rudimentary hose cart and salt water pump at the ferry landing, and the ferryboats and smaller vessels relied on sand-filled pails stored on board. The municipal water supply was insufficient for fire-

*In many respects the Sausalito Volunteer Fire Department was like a fraternal organization, dedicated to service and camaraderie. In 1909 this hose cart company at Richardson and Second Streets consisted of: left to right, Walter Dreschler, Sam Marion, G. Faulkes, Joe Quadros, Tony Veira, P. Golthwaith, Ray Renner, Jack Elliott Jr., G. Gill, E. Payne. The young lady wreathed in flowers on the cart is the mascot, a niece of Fire Chief Jewett.*

*Sausalito's original firehouse was next to the San Francisco Yacht Club on the site of the tank house shown here (left), c. 1902. In the same scene taken in 1983 (above), the old firehouse is the gable-roofed building across the street and slightly south of the yacht club building.*

fighting. Before 1914 it was common practice to shut off domestic water from 7 a.m. to evening due to short supply.

It was decided by the self-appointed committee to levy a special property tax within a new fire district to raise $1,000,000. A new horse-drawn Babcock steam pumper was purchased in March, 1888, in anticipation of future tax revenues. But too many property owners within the proposed district felt the assessment was too steep, and the vote to establish a fire department failed by six votes in June, 1888. It would be another sixteen years before Sausalito again attempted to establish a permanent fire department.

By the turn of the century there was again growing concern over lack of an organized fire department in Sausalito. For many residents however, *ad hoc* volunteer companies seemed perfectly adequate. During the debate on incorporation in 1893, public opinion held that paid fire departments were an unnecessary burden on taxpayers and that even permanent volunteers were superfluous. The big fire of July 4, 1893, that raced unchecked through Sausalito's business district changed many minds concerning the need for firefighting equipment and trained men. By 1904 the Board of Trustees was concerned enough to take some positive action. Arthur Jewett, the blacksmith, was appointed the town's first Fire Marshall. Along with his title, Jewett also got the job of building the hose carts.

The first hose cart station was established in a shed at the Sausalito Land & Ferry Company equipment yard. For this prime location at the ferry landing the city was charged twenty dollars a month. Still the carts were manned by disorganized volunteers.

Because the 1906 San Francisco fire convinced the Sausalito Board of Trustees that it was time to get serious about fire protection, they enacted an ordinance in 1909 creating a permanent Sausalito Volunteer Fire Department. Arthur Jewett was appointed Fire Chief at twenty-five dollars a month, and five more hose cart stations were established. The city bought a fire wagon and horses and by 1914 made plans for an actual firehouse. Residents were informed of the new fire alarm system, utilizing church bells to call volunteers from their homes.

The new station, housing both firewagon and horses, was built next to the San Francisco Yacht Club on Water Street (it was moved across the street in 1931, where the building stands today). To get the most out of its investment, the city later added jail cells in the station house, and to keep the chief busy when there were no fires, he was made official dogcatcher and poundmaster. There was never a shortage of stray dogs and horses wandering through backyards.

*This Huckleberry Finn is really Russell McGowan, a lifelong Sausalito resident at his waterfront home, foot of Napa Street c. 1910. At his feet is a Waldo Pointer, as the breed became known in later years, named for Waldo Point, the place where many waterfront dogs originated.*

The foot of Napa Street has always been a center of maritime activity. When the first pier was built there is not recorded, but there has been a Napa Street pier of some sort for over 100 years. In the 1870s and 1880s Italian fishing families lived there and built their traditional feluccas on the beach. After the turn of the century, a few arks and pole houses remained but most fishermen worked out of San Francisco by this time. The area was purchased by the Oceanic Boatyard Company, and boatbuilding on bigger scale began. One by one the arks were demolished or moved as the waterfront around Napa Street took on a more industrial character.

*Boatbuilder and fishermen Stephen Brigante (right) and family pose on a newly launched felucca near Napa Street, c. 1913. Brigante sold his property near the foot of Turney Street, which he called the Atlantic Boat Building Plant, to James Herbert Madden in 1915.*

*Napa Street, c. 1914. The boatyard of Crichton and Arques, who leased the property from Oceanic Boatyard Company, dominates the scene with the lumber schooner* Advance *flanked by stern-wheelers,* Grace Barton *and* Phoenix.

97

*Mr. Peters and Mr. Olsen (above) pose proudly in front of their respective places of business on Water Street. This photo was used in a promotional brochure in 1911 called "Sausalito, Geneva of America," in which the utility poles and the trash in the street were carefully retouched out of the scene.*

*The sign in Druggist Olsen's window reads: "FREE! Try a bottle of Pabst Extract, the best tonic and get a beautiful 1911 America Girl Art Calendar Free."*

*Victor Trouette, left, son of French immigrants Paul and Marianna Trouette, was born in Sausalito in 1885. In 1916 he moved his meat market into Jean Baptiste Baraty's building (12-20 Princess Street). Trouette is shown here in 1917 with clerk George Bergman.*

*Thomas Young, (below right), owned this lot next to the Baraty Building on Princess Street, where he ran the Western Feed & Fuel Company. He built a storefront here in 1913 (28 Princess Street). The wagon is standing on the site of Princess Court.*

98

*Looking north (above) along electrified but as yet unpaved Water Street from Princess Street in 1910. On the right is the sales office for the Sausalito Land & Ferry Company, built in 1902 on the site of the first ferry landing. Upstairs was the first Sausalito Public Library and reading room, installed in 1906. Next to it is Charlie Becker's store and newstand with Fred Fiedler's general store beyond that. At the far left is the welcome arch that gave El Portal its name and the plaza beyond. Water Street merchants chipped in to construct the arch in 1908 as a welcome for the Great White Fleet. Over the years the arch deteriorated, and in 1915 it was pulled down as a public menace.*

*This brick storefront with cast-iron detailing was built by Charles Becker in 1897 on the east side of Water Street at Princess Street. In this 1910 photograph (left) with Becker and an unidentified little girl standing in front, the window sign reads: "I. E. Noyes, successor to C. H. Becker's News Depot." The Beckers lived in a tiny house at 52 Princess Street which for years bore the sign, "Klein aber Mein," small but mine. The ferryboat* Tamalpais *can be seen at the far left. The Becker Building today, above, has changed little.*

*Interior of the Marin Fruit Company in October, 1923. On the left is Yee Tock Chee, known as Willie Yee, whose kindness and beneficence endeared him to generations of Sausalitans. On the right is Wing Mow Lung who started the business then returned to China.*

*Marin Fruit Company today. It is essentially unchanged since the 1920s.*

Yee Tock Chee came from Ch'ang On village in Canton to San Francisco around 1918. Following the traditional pattern of Chinese immigrants of the period, he found work as a houseboy, laborer, dishwasher, and cook. His cousin, Wing Mow Lung who ran a small grocery store on Water Street in Sausalito hired Yee and taught him the grocery business. When Wing returned to China, he turned the business over to Yee Tock Chee, now known as Willie Yee. In the decades that followed, Willie Yee became an institution in Sausalito. He worked hard to serve his customers, providing the best produce available, delivering free to hillside homes, and dispensing good cheer along with his merchandise. During the Depression, he extended credit to families when cash was scarce, often carrying people on his books for months. His concern for Sausalito, his neighbors and customers through hard times resulted in customer loyalty that helped Marin Fruit Company survive in the age of supermarkets. Today the little waterfront park at the foot of Princess Street, near the Marin Fruit Company, is named Yee Tock Chee Park, in memory of Willie Yee.

*Old Town in 1905. Newly completed South School is the largest building near the center of the photo. In front of it, between Third and Fourth Streets are four identical new cottages, the nearest thing Old Town ever had to a housing tract.*

*Sunrise in Old Town (above right), c. 1906 a remarkable glass-plate photograph by William Sutherland. Two square-riggers ride at anchor between Angel Island in the background and the Walhalla, with its sign advertising clam chowder for ten cents.*

Sausalito's business district developed pretty much the way Sausalito Land & Ferry Company directors had envisioned. Princess and Water Street merchants catered to the Hill residents and railroad and ferryboat passengers. Caledonia Street shops met most needs of New Town residents. Old Town, however, was primarily residential and developed more slowly. In 1884 a small storefront with living quarters above was built at Richardson and Second Streets that evolved into the Golden Gate Market by the early 1920s. It served early Old Town residents and the quartermasters from the military reservation.

This store plus the waterfront saloons and one or two short-lived shops were the extent of commercial development in Old Town until the 1920s. All growth, residential and commercial, during the early twentieth century was dependent on ferryboat and railroad traffic. Despite claims that the town was the "Geneva of America," Sausalito was irrevocably a transportation terminal, tightly linked to the fortunes or misfortunes of the North Pacific Coast Railroad.

On the morning of April 18, 1906, Sausalitans awoke to an earthquake stronger than any in memory. Electric wires snapped, brick chimneys toppled, dishes and crockery were shattered. But Sausalito rode out the big quake with relatively little damage. There were only minor injuries and fortunately no fires.

By that afternoon many residents were learning the awful fate of San Francisco, hidden under a pall of smoke. The morning ferryboats had made their regular runs to San Francisco but returned jammed with refugees from the spreading holocaust. In the weeks following the earthquake and fire, Sausalito, like other cities around the Bay, became a refuge for many homeless San Franciscans.

*Richardson Street (right) in the foreground and Fourth Street leading uphill to South School at left, c. 1907. Another row of cottages has been built below the school. Following the San Francisco fire, Sausalito experienced a population increase, although the anticipated real-estate boom did not live up to real-estate speculators' hopes. Surprisingly, almost all the houses in this photograph still exist, including the one at Richardson and West Streets from which this photo was taken.*

An economic recession in 1893 created a shift of power and reorganization of stockholders of the North Pacific Coast Railroad. With an infusion of new capital, a new train shed was constructed in Sausalito wide enough to enclose four trains at once and for the first time provide sheltered access for the increasing number of passengers. Although freight revenue declined in the 1890s, passenger revenue increased as more people settled in Marin County and commuted to San Francisco. A second track was added between Sausalito and Mill Valley to accommodate the growing number of daily trains.

In spite of increasing patronage, the North Pacific Coast Railroad continued to be plagued with financial problems. With generous backing by Southern Pacific, the North Shore Railroad bought out the troubled line in 1902,

*The Sausalito railroad and ferry terminal in 1903, after standard-gauge, electric commuter trains had been added. The freight wharf is to the left, where the ferry* Sausalito *is in the slip. To the right is the new terminal building.*

*The freight wharf is to the left, where the ferry* Tamalpais *is in the slip. Next to it are the little sternwheeler* Lagunitas *and the* Cazadero. *Approaching the terminal building is the* Sausalito.

*The little steamer* Requa *was a Northwestern Pacific shuttle between Sausalito and Tiburon beginning in 1909. Two years later* Requa *burned at her moorings in Belvedere lagoon. Rebuilt as the* Marin, *she continued in service and was by firsthand accounts, a very seaworthy and pleasant little craft.*

promising big changes for Marin County rail service. And changes there were. The first move was to add broad-gauge electrified interurban trains using existing roadbeds. Electric "third rail" trains were in service on the East Coast, primarily in New York's subways and on elevated inner city lines in New York and Chicago. But Marin County's system was the first electrified "third rail" interurban system in the nation. The third rail, carrying electric current to the trains, was installed alongside the existing narrow-gauge tracks, and a fourth rail was added so both broad- and narrow-gauge trains could run over the same trackage.

The eight-year-old train shed in Sausalito was pulled down as part of an extensive redesign of the ferry wharf. Tracks were rearranged and a new, two-story terminal building constructed, with two-level loading slips for the double-ended ferryboats. The North Shore Railroad also filled the "Pond" next to the terminal and presented Sausalito with a new plaza (today's Plaza Viña del Mar).

New ferries were ordered—the huge Cazadero and the freight hauler Lagunitas—and the eight-year-old Sausalito was modernized. The railcars were refurbished, and the old, hodgepodge colors, some yellow, some green or orange, were repainted a bright red. Even the steam passenger locomotives were painted red, with gold lettering. They made a fine sight pulling into the new Sausalito terminal with its stone facade and tidy, landscaped plaza.

But like its many predecessors, the North Shore Railroad overspent, and it too became the target of acquisition in 1904, scarcely after the improvements were completed. Still seeking control of all railroading in northern California (and elsewhere), Southern Pacific took over the North Shore and the California Northwestern Railroad and applied the North Shore name to both. The battle between the rail giants, Southern Pacific and Santa Fe, for control of the small local lines reached a fever pitch around the turn of the century. Finally, after concluding that it would be unprofitable to operate two competitive rail complexes in northern California, the two giants cooperated to form a single new entity in 1907 called the Northwestern Pacific Railroad, putting an end to the confusing guessing game of which railroad owned which rail line. The new company encompassed most of the small lines between San Francisco and Eureka, including the old North Shore that served Sausalito.

The Northwestern Pacific Railroad with its familiar redwood tree symbol emblazoned on rail cars and ferryboats continued passenger service to Sausalito until 1941 and maintained freight service until the last train pulled out of Sausalito in 1971. Today, with buildings constructed across the old roadbed in some places, the only vestiges of Sausalito's railroad era are a few sections of track, rotted pilings where thousands of commuters once boarded ferryboats, a few artifacts, and many memories.

*Switching cars in Sausalito was made easier in 1910 with this new engine. Standing second from left, c. 1917 is Henry Clouette, Sr., and fourth from left is Bill Wosser.*

*This young lady, photographed in the summer of 1898, would like us to think she is about to dive into the cool waters of the Russian River from her rowboat, the* Great Eastern. *The hills behind her have by this time been stripped of usable timber. The former lumber towns above Duncan Mills on the river, Monte Rio, Guerneville, and Rio Nido became popular destinations for weekend campers and vacationers. The Russian River again became a source of revenue for the railroad.*

"The Crookedest Railroad in the World" was the Mt. Tamalpais Scenic Railway. The slogan referred not to the company's fiscal policies but to its tracks, which twisted up Mount Tamalpais. In the 1870s the slopes around Mt. Tamalpais were becoming resort areas for the wealthy. Summer homes and small farms for weekend leisure brought relief from San Francisco's hectic pace for those who could afford it. The ferry/train trip via Sausalito was a pleasant, relatively quick one. In 1896 the Mt. Tamalpais Scenic Railway brought the visual delights of the legendary mountain to the multitudes. Sightseers could board the narrow-gauge train at Mill Valley's station and chug slowly up the tortuous mountain tracks to Tamalpais Tavern, 2,400 feet above San Francisco Bay. This popular attraction lasted well into the automobile era and was abandoned in 1930.

*Engine Number 4 of the Mount Tamalpais and Muir Woods Railway pauses for the photographer below the summit of Mt. Tamalpais in October, 1918.*

The Thomas Frost home, above on Sunshine Avenue, built in 1901.
By 1910 automobile tires as well as buggy wheels made tracks
on Sausalito's unpaved streets. The automobile was becoming
a threat to the railroad as more and more people acquired
horseless carriages. The Creede family used their Model T
Ford even when visiting friends across town. The snapshop
at top center was taken c. 1912 when the Creedes visited the
Thomas Frost home on Sunshine Avenue.

The Crossroads, left, the intersection of Bulkley Avenue,
Harrison Avenue, and San Carlos Avenue. It was a
difficult intersection to negotiate with a horse and buggy, but
autos had an easier time of it, except when it rained.
This photo was taken about the time Mrs. Arabelle Mays in
her 1912 Elmore became Sausalito's first woman automobile driver.

"F. W. Finn of San Carlos Avenue is building
a garage for his new Studebaker, a recent
acquisition."
"E. H. Daniel of San Carlos Avenue is building
a double garage on his property."
—Sausalito News

*The Wossers and their Model T Ford, 1914, with one of the younger family members at the wheel.*

*Grain merchant, world traveler, and sportsman Billy Berg paid $10,000 to have this house (below) constructed on Santa Rosa Avenue in 1905. It is visible in the Crossroads photograph at top center. The gregarious Berg, a native of Bavaria, had a concrete wine cellar built beneath the ten-room house.*

The Creede family and their Model T Ford (c. 1912)
were camping companions. Marin County was filled
with lovely, uncrowded campsites. All that was needed
was a trusty automobile, tent, camp stove, and whatever
else could be lashed to the auto.

*Santa Cruz boardwalk and beach, c. 1913. The Creedes took their camera with them on weekend trips. The automobile opened new horizons for middle-class families who traditionally did very little traveling. The sign reads: "Japanese Parasols, For Sale and To Rent."*

*Some preferred more civilized camping. Identified only as Fred and his mother, this family enjoys a permanent tent platform on the slopes of Mt. Tamalpais, c. 1910.*

*Girls basketball team at Mount Tamalpais Union High School, 1910. The young people on these pages were about to experience an event that would remain clearly etched in their memory: the 1915 Panama Pacific International Exposition in San Francisco.*

*Classmates at Mount Tamalpais Union High School, c. 1912. Edith Romer Ritchie of Sausalito, third from left.*

*From the Ritchie album: off to college,* c. 1912.

*May Day Parade, Kentfield, c. 1910. Sausalito children were widely travelled compared to those in inland small towns. The ferries, trains, and later the automobile provided the means to visit San Francisco, the East Bay, and other Marin County towns with comparative ease.*

*May 1, 1914. The big day has arrived! The Sausalito Maypole Dancers twenty-four strong, accompanied by a contingent of twenty flag bearers and a drummer boy, are off to the Phoenix Fete at the Panama Pacific International Exposition, then under construction. The event was a competition among Bay Area children who could barely contain their excitement over the upcoming exposition. The tour buses shown here whisked them from the Ferry Building in San Francisco to the exposition grounds. Presumably they did not have to pay the rather exorbitant one dollar per head fare for the bus ride.*

*The children returned with a silver cup for their efforts and as the* Sausalito News *reported, "pleasant memories which can be carried in each little heart through the years to come."*

Plans for an international exposition to celebrate the opening of the Panama Canal began as early as 1904 when the canal project was started. By 1910 competition for the privilege of hosting the fair had narrowed to San Francisco and New Orleans, each working hard to sell its case before Congress. Louisiana passed a bond issue in 1910 to raise over $7,000,000 as a contribution toward financing the exposition. California waged a successful campaign to pass two bond issues totaling $17,000,000, thus underwriting the entire estimated cost. Congress was persuaded that the logical site for this world's fair was San Francisco, a port city rebuilt from the devastation of earthquake and fire in 1906. It was a city that would benefit enormously from the Panama Canal and would welcome the opportunity to demonstrate to the world that California was now a leader in international commerce.

By the time the fair opened on February 20, 1915, many of the twenty-five nations represented were at war. California seemed a million miles from the trenches of European battlefields, and the jeweled city, like the magic land of Oz, bedazzled and captivated fairgoers. Sausalito and other bay cities were well represented in the parade through San Francisco on the opening day of the Panama-Pacific International Exposition. For San Francisco, the roaring success of the exposition signified that the City had indeed risen from the ashes of 1906 and was ready to take its place again on the roster of great cities.

*The Scintillator: forty-eight searchlights manned by U.S. Marines on the pier in San Francisco's marina (site of St. Francis Yacht Club). A light drill, designed by William Ryan, created a rainbow effect, an artificial Aurora Borealis that bounced multicolored lights off the summer fog in San Francisco Bay. If fog was lacking, the lights played on steam clouds generated by a locomotive stationed on the outer wall of the yacht harbor.*

*Electricity for the Scintillator and all the other lighting for the exposition was supposed to come via submarine cable from a new Pacific Gas and Electric Company substation built high on the ridge above Old Town. Construction of the substation was delayed, however, and the exposition had come and gone by the time the building and lines were completed in October, 1916.*

*The Panama Pacific at night with the Scintillator in action, a multicolored wonderland.*

*The Court of the Universe looking toward the Arch of the Rising Sun. In the immense scale of the exposition buildings, the elephants on either side of the arch beneath their 100 foot flagpoles are barely visible. Atop the arch is a group of elephants and camels symbolizing the nations of the Orient. Opposite this was the Arch of the Setting Sun, surmounted with beasts from Western nations. There were also two elephants in front of that arch, but their fate is unknown.*

The exposition complex was built on mud flats at today's Marina District, north of Lombard Street. Entering a main gate at Scott and Lombard Streets, the public was invited into a dream world of fantastic palaces and courtyards, colossal domes, and broad promenades lined with statuary. Designed by such prestigious architectural firms as McKim, Meade and White, and Bliss and Faville, the structures were steel skeletons covered with concrete and stucco colored to simulate Italian travertine—at least at a distance. They were not intended to be permanent, but to last for only one year. When the exposition closed on December 4, 1915, the statuary and detailing were sold off, buildings demolished, and the land cleared and sold as real-estate subdivisions. A few of the ornate "palaces" were sold intact and turned up in cities around the bay, recycled for other uses. Only the Palace of Fine Arts, designed by Bernard Maybeck, survived intact on site. It was restored in 1967.

Architect William Faville, who had designed much of the fair, was then a Sausalito resident. As a gift to Sausalito, Faville purchased one of the two small Italianate fountains he had designed for the Half Dome of the Palace of Education, and two flagpoles with elephant bases that had stood in front of the Triumphal Arch of the Rising Sun in the Court of the Universe. In early 1916 he had them delivered to Sausalito by ferry and installed in Depot Park, the little plaza in front of the ferry terminal. The fountain and elephant flagpoles were an immediate hit with residents, who dubbed the elephants Jumbo and Pee Wee.

By 1926 time had taken a toll on the exposition relics. The weight of the 100-foot-tall Oregon Pine flagpoles had all but shattered the elephants. The poles were removed for safety. In December, 1935, a workman cleaning the elephants climbed atop Jumbo, causing the head to crash to the sidewalk. The *Sausalito News* reported that the

*The elephants and fountain installed in their new home, Sausalito's plaza, 1916. The new Sausalito Hotel, which replaced the Arbordale, is in background. The Northwestern Pacific terminal building is at far left.*

*One of the elephants in Plaza Viña Del Mar today.*

entire front half of the weathered elephant was in ruins, exposing the rotted wood flagpole base "poor Jumbo has been trying to digest all these years." William Faville, now seventy, came to the rescue. At his own expense, he had the elephants replaced with new castings made from Pee Wee, and the tops modified into candelabras with electric lights. Broken portions of the fountain were replaced and much of the plumbing redone. The new elephants, made of more durable material, are again showing the ravages of time, and someday will require recasting. The fountain, deteriorating badly, was completely recast in 1977, thanks to citizen contributions, as part of Sausalito's Bicentennial Project.

The elephants have become an appropriate symbol of Sausalito. Now, decades after the Panama-Pacific International Exposition, visitors to Sausalito often ask, "Why elephants?" to which the only reply is, "Why not elephants?"

The Panama Pacific International Exposition brought many first-time visitors to Sausalito. Local merchants responded by hiring barkers to greet passengers arriving by ferry. A resident recalls that one "chirped like a chicken" to get attention, and sold hot tomales from a cart. Others wore sandwich boards advertising restaurants and saloons. One cried out as passengers disembarked, "This way to the Miramar Cafe!"

The first Miramar Cafe, built on pilings off the foot of Johnson Street was advertised as "a family resort, with hot and cold fresh and salt water tub baths, accommodating fourteen people at one time." It had a large dining room designed to "cater to the trade of the better element." It only lasted one year before being destroyed by fire. Rebuilt in 1912, the second Miramar was strictly a cafe although it was architecturally more flamboyant than its predecessor. In October, 1915, the Miramar burned again, and its owner was charged with arson. It was never rebuilt.

Out-of-town guests at the Miramar saw Sausalito as a pleasant escape from the ardors of city life. To them Sausalito was a charming, carefree village. But to many residents there was a fear that the charm was in danger.

The Sausalito Woman's Club was organized in 1913 by a group of Sausalito women whose goal was to "promote and preserve the beauty of Sausalito and to support other worthy causes which benefit the people of Sausalito." This followed an incident two years earlier in which several women living near the First Presbyterian Church on Bulkley Avenue attempted to save a row of cypress trees that were being cut down. They arrived in time to save one tree, now known as the "Founder's Tree." The club was incorporated March 13, 1916, but as yet members had no permanent clubhouse. In 1917 the president of the Bank of Sausalito, Frederick A. Robbins donated a site on Central Avenue in memory of his wife, the late Grace McGregor Robbins.

From the beginning club members had worked diligently to raise money and by 1913 had accumulated $2,000 in the building fund. The club commissioned California architect Julia Morgan to design a suitable clubhouse. Morgan was the first woman to receive a master's

*The second Miramar Cafe, c. 1915.*

CHRISTIANSEN

*The Sausalito Woman's Club building, completed in 1918, was designed by the highly esteemed architect Julia Morgan.*

degree from the *Ecole des Beaux Arts* in Paris and the first woman to earn an engineering degree from the University of California (in 1894). She produced a design of splendid proportions that stands today as a monument to her talents.

The final cost of the clubhouse, however, was over $5,000, a considerable sum in 1918. Raising the additional money caused a controversy among members whose interest in fund raising for the club was overshadowed by a more pressing need: the support of American men fighting in Europe. The president at the time, Clara Earl Lanagan related the dilemma to her husband, Major James A. Lanagan with the Anti-Air Craft Service in France. He replied that he would be "greatly comforted in the trenches" if he knew events at home were "proceeding in a normal way." That settled the controversy and the money was raised, with Frederick Robbins matching each dollar. On September 5, 1918, the first meeting of the Sausalito Woman's Club was held in the new clubhouse.

CHRISTIANSEN

119

One hundred and forty one men from Sausalito enlisted in 1917 when America declared war on Germany. The draft took many more in 1918.

The Northwestern Pacific Railroad participated in selling Liberty Bonds.
This train publicized the Fourth Victory Loan in 1918 in an effort to raise funds for the final push.

*The innocence and optimism of small town America in 1917 when the nation entered World War I is personified in this graduation portrait of Margaret Ammerman (Mrs. Frank Rossman).*

*Eighteen-year-old Russell McGowan (see page 96)
of the 67th Coast Artillery arrived home from France
with his regiment in March, 1919. Six young men
from Sausalito died in France, a small number given
the scale of the Great War, but their loss had a
profound impact in the small town of Sausalito.*

*Liberty Bond salesmen drink a toast to victory in front
of Ray Ellis' Caledonia Street store after a hard
day's work. 1918.*

*Waiting for the ferryboat, c. 1919. Following World War I Sausalito had the appearance of a turn of the century town. Automobiles and paved streets, however, are signs of the times. The small boy with his lollypop, far left, has chosen a fire hydrant as a perch rather than the jagged stone fence surrounding the plaza. Resident's complaints about the uncomfortable seating resulted in the addition of a smooth concrete cap. The lady in the foreground reading a newspaper must be made of sterner stuff.*

The decade ahead would bring big changes in Sausalito. By 1919 there was already considerable talk about a bridge across the Golden Gate. The automobile was becoming a nuisance in the opinion of some residents. Also in 1919 the nation went dry.

On January 16, 1920, national prohibition went into effect. The Eighteenth Amendment to the Constitution prohibiting the manufacture, sale, or transportation of intoxicating liquors was given legislative "teeth" by passage of the Prohibition Enforcement Act, or "Volstead Act," that defined intoxicating liquor as "anything with more than 0.5% alcohol." Sausalito's saloons and liquor stores closed; beer, wine, and whiskey disappeared from grocery store shelves as California and the nation began the thirteen-year experiment that ended in repeal.

At first, prohibition had very little impact on Sausalito. Most people who were so inclined had stocked up on their favorite beverages, and those with access to grain soon learned the brewer's art. The saloons reopened as "Soft Drink Parlors," where it was usually possible to get a little something to liven up a seltzer. Mason's Distillery in Sausalito, a major producer of whiskey, underwent some worrisome moments until its role under the Volstead Act was determined. Mason's continued to manufacture alcohol under federal license for medicinal and industrial purposes. By 1925 the Mason By-Products Company was producing 2 million gallons of denatured alcohol per year, nearly one-sixth of all the alcohol produced in the country.

In the early 1920s, Sausalito had only two policemen, making enforcement of prohibition impossible. It was about as easy to get a drink in Sausalito as it had been before prohibition. As in most of the country, it became fashionable and somewhat daring to visit "speakeasies" or underground saloons and to know a bootlegger by his first name. One Sausalito resident recalls that as a boy he made pocket money by collecting empty liquor bottles that had washed up on Marin beaches and selling them to local contacts. The bottles would probably turn up the next day with new labels proclaiming the contents to be "genuine" twelve-year-old Scotch.

Canada, where sale of alcholic beverages was still legal, was a major source of bootleg whiskey during prohibition. Marin County with its miles of unguarded beaches became a popular landing zone for whiskey smuggled in

123

*Contraband alcohol, or what appears to be alcohol, is dumped into Richardson's Bay. Everyone got into the act: left to right, Fire Chief Charles Loriano, Judge Paul Helmore, Councilman Manuel Ignacio, Police Chief James McGowan, Traffic Office Manuel Menotti, and two unidentified onlookers.*

from Vancouver or for "moonshine" disguised as Canadian whiskey or Mexican rum. Soon Sausalito was the funnel through which bootleg alcohol passed to its destination in San Francisco's speakeasies. Knowing that a shortage of federal agents making random searches of vehicles on the San Francisco side of the bay meant little chance of getting caught, bootleggers brazenly loaded their liquor-filled autos and trucks onto ferryboats in Sausalito.

Because the prohibition law was unpopular, local authorities received little help in enforcing it from residents. When a speakeasy or hidden still was raided, it was usually because the bootleggers got too bold. The Soft Drink Parlor Walhalla was raided in 1921. There had been reports of considerable nightime activity at a trap door leading from Walhalla's floor to the bay beneath, where small boats could be hidden among the pilings. Annie Lowder, proprietor of the Walhalla, was carried off kicking and screaming after agents found 478 quarts of home-brew and "a large quantity of jackass brandy with

a vigorous kick." The Sausalito Cash Grocery on Princess Street was raided in 1926 by Town Marshall Al O'Connor and Officer Manuel Menotti after neighbors complained of customers coming and going all night long. Sure enough, a small-time bootlegging operation had exceeded the bounds of propriety and called attention to itself.

Most people treated prohibition lightly. Alcohol was served at most social events in private homes, and often at club meetings. Jokes circulated about the latest "imports" and about the unprecedented number of drug store prescriptions for high alcoholic content cough medicine. But the lightheartedness diminished as incidents of serious illness and death from "bum booze" increased. An even more sinister side to prohibition developed in the mid-1920s when organized crime made bootlegging its number one activity. The Volstead Act was a dream come true for big-time gangsters. It drove an indispensable consumer product underground, creating a bonanza for criminals who had the money to buy and deliver large quantities of alcohol.

*Mason's Distillery (left), Sausalito's major manufacturer since 1892 when it was opened as Mason's Malt Whisky Distilling Company. It became the American Distilling Company the day prohibition ended. The County Road passes in front and winds around Waldo Point, far left in this photo taken in the mid-1920s. The Northwestern Pacific Railroad tracks run straight across the tidal marsh. The distillery burned in 1963, and the site today is occupied by Whisky Springs, a condominium project.*

*Sausalito Mayor Webb Mahaffy, center, and two hunting companions somewhere in West Marin, c. 1930. Since prohibition is in effect, the bottle about to be passed undoubtedly contains lemonade.*

*The Sylva Mansion where Baby Face Nelson is reputed to have lived. Built in 1897 by Adolph Sylva, who as mayor in 1900 supported poolroom gambling in Sausalito. After his defeat in 1902 by the "anti-poolies," Sylva dropped out of local politics. In 1907 N. P. Yost acquired the property at a trustee's sale. It was converted to a boarding house in the 1930s and today consists of several apartments, although the exterior is essentially unchanged.*

A national underground network of alcohol distribution developed, with the local user knowing only his immediate supplier, the friendly neighborhood bootlegger. Increasingly determined to crack down on gangsterism, federal agents arrested as many links in the chain of distribution as possible, often with some surprising results. Sausalito's mayor, John Herbert Madden, learned first-hand about the federal crackdown on prohibition violators.

On Friday, July 3, 1924, the fuel-supply ship *Comet,* suspected of being a "rumrunner," caught fire at the Union Oil docks in San Francisco and exploded. A badly burned survivor tipped federal agents to a complex boot-legging operation involving dozens of men. Within days of the explosion, an investigation led to a round up of suspects, including Sausalito's Herb Madden. A partner in the Sausalito boatbuilding firm of Madden and Lewis as well as mayor, Madden was charged along with seventeen others with conspiracy to violate the Volstead Act. He was accused of repairing the vessel *Principio* in San Pedro in 1924 with the knowledge that the ship was a known "rumrunner" owned by San Francisco bootlegger Joe Parente. Madden denied the charge, claiming that his boatyard repaired all manner of boats including Coast

Guard patrol vessels, and that in many cases he did not personally examine the vessels.

The *Principio,* like the ill-fated *Comet,* had been part of a scheme to smuggle Canadian liquor into San Francisco. Herb Madden was hired as an expert shipfitter to work on the *Principio* and according to the federal indictment must have seen that the vessel was rigged as a "rumrunner." He was found guilty of conspiracy in 1926, sentenced to two years' imprisonment at McNeil Island, Washington, and fined $5,000. Madden continued to profess innocence in the affair; nonetheless, he served fifteen months of the sentence before his release. He was again elected to the City Council and in 1936 chosen as Mayor of Sausalito.

---

One of the easiest ways to make money during Prohibition was as a driver. After making the right connections and receiving instructions (spoken, never written), a driver would appear at the designated place and time with his automobile or truck. Often it was San Rafael or Novato, where liquor had been transported from the desolate beaches of west Marin after being unloaded from "rumrunners" or fast boats in the dead of night. The

126

*Constable and Traffic Officer Manuel Menotti, c. 1930. He was elected constable in 1926 and served until his death in 1937. Dedicated, efficient, and extremely well liked, Menotti gained wide recognition as a peace officer. News of his death in a traffic accident near Gilroy stunned Sausalito. He is well remembered to this day.*

driver, with a load of several cases of bootleg "hooch," would head straight for the Sausalito ferry terminal. There the truck was driven aboard a ferryboat bound for San Francisco. If he evaded the random searches of vehicles at the Ferry Building or Hyde Street, the driver delivered the contraband to his contact and was paid in cash.

A Sausalito resident who made his living that way in the early thirties was John Paul Chase, who had established a reputation for toughness and reliability as a bootlegger. In the summer of 1932, through his Marin connections, he met a young man who needed work. Chase befriended the quiet, unassuming youth. Lester Gillis, barely five feet, four inches tall, looked even younger than his twenty-three years. Chase found a room for Gillis near his home on Turney Street, in the old Sylva mansion, now converted to a boarding house. Gillis, his nineteen-year-old wife Helen, and their three-year-old son moved into the quiet neighborhood. John Chase learned that Gillis, far different than his mild demeanor indicated, was an escaped convict from Illinois. He was a bank robber, known in Chicago as George Nelson, one of several aliases he used. He was also known there by his childhood nickname, "Baby Face."

Gillis, a hardened criminal and experienced gunman, apparently fooled his Sausalito neighbors and his employer at the Walhalla, where he worked as a part-time bartender. Even his neighbor on Turney Street, constable Manuel Menotti, didn't suspect that the quiet young man was the dangerous Baby Face Nelson.

Chase took an apartment in San Rafael and had a rented garage in Novato where he kept the trucks used in his expanding bootlegging operation. He and Gillis became familiar customers at a small cafe in San Rafael, where during their chats with the counterman they made no mention of Lester Gillis teaching Johnny Chase how to handle a Thompson submachine gun out on the deserted beach at Point Reyes. Gillis grew restless in Sausalito and through San Francisco gangster Joe Parente was introduced to John Dillinger's gang. After a series of bank robberies and the murder of a federal agent during an at-

tempt to capture Dillinger in Wisconsin, Gillis gained nationwide notoriety as "Baby Face Nelson," feared even by Dillinger himself. Chicago became too hot for Gillis and he returned to California, in 1934, where he again met John Chase in Sausalito.

After several weeks had passed, during which Gillis, alias Baby Face Nelson, had been harbored by several Bay Area and Reno contacts, Chase and Gillis headed for Chicago. Accompanying them were several gang members, Helen Gillis, and her young son. Life on the road, camping out in makeshift tents and avoiding restaurants was not the glamorous life depicted in the slick magazines of that period. The "romantic" era of bank robbers was rapidly coming to an end. Dillinger was dead. Bonnie and Clyde, Pretty Boy Floyd, and countless lesser-known bandits were dead or behind bars. Federal agents also soon caught up with Baby Face Nelson.

He was cornered one night with his wife Helen and Johnny Chase outside a resort near Chicago. After a furious but brief gunbattle, two agents lay dead, and the fatally wounded Baby Face Nelson was sped away by Chase and Helen Gillis. The two dumped his bullet-riddled body by the roadside and went their separate ways. Chase was captured near Mt. Shasta in California in December, 1934, and later sentenced to life imprisonment for murder in the Chicago shootout. Helen Gillis was taken shortly thereafter and given a light sentence as an accomplice, for harboring a fugitive. Sausalito's constable Manuel Menotti flew to Shasta City to assist in the identification and capture of Chase when it was learned he was hiding there. Because of the numerous friends and "business" acquaintances of John Paul Chase, Sausalitans who knew Chase and Gillis were reluctant to talk about the episode for years afterward. Ironically, John Paul Chase was sent to Alcatraz, the new federal penitentiary, where he could look across the bay to Sausalito. He served the longest term on Alcatraz of any convicted felon — twenty-six years. After seven additional years at Leavenworth, he was paroled. He died in 1973.

*S*ausalito residents depended on the railroad and the ferryboats for transportation, but like everyone else in the country they fell in love with the automobile. As early as 1902, enough automobiles were clanking and chugging along unpaved Marin County roads to cause concern. It was generally considered that only pedestrians had anything to fear from the new horseless carriages. No one dreamed that these mechanical marvels would one day threaten the very existence of powerful and graceful vessels like the ferryboats *Sausalito* and *Tamalpais* or of the fast new electric commuter trains. Owners of motor cars praised them with an almost fanatic fervor. They formed automobile clubs and replaced the traditional peaceful Sunday picnic with the "run," a dusty endurance trek over rutted wagon roads to some almost inaccessible spot.

The Sausalito Board of Trustees proposed a tax on automobiles in 1902, and a town license fee; it also recommended a strictly enforced speed limit in Sausalito of six miles per hour. The ferryboat captains grudgingly allowed a few autos to be transported across the bay as freight, but only if gasoline was drained from them first. The half-dozen or more autos were pulled on and off the ferries by mule team and were carried only on a "space permitting" basis.

By 1903 automobiles in Marin were considered a nuisance by many residents, some of whom signed a petition for an ordinance prohibiting the use of automobiles on Marin County roads. It said in part: "The automobile can never be anything but a toy for the wealthy. It is one of the most important inventions of the age, and has undoubtedly come among us to stay. But, the automobile is a dangerous piece of mechanism and there should be drastic legislation passed to regulate it. Marin County is, first, last and always, a horse loving and horse keeping county and would attract many more residents were it to become known that here at last there is a refuge from the constantly increasing menace of the horseless carriage. The present risk to life involved in the use of the horseless carriage is not so much to those who ride as to those in the vicinity. It is admitted that the machine has a place, but that its place is not in Marin County."

Words alone could not stem the tide. With the advent, around 1910, of relatively low-cost automobiles, principally the Model T Ford, it became clear even to the most stubborn foe that the automobile was indeed here to stay. The ubiquitous "Tin Lizzie" brought about a call for better roads everywhere in Marin. Sausalito residents who wanted to keep autos at their hillside homes needed paved roads to make the steep grades passable. Merchants abandoned horses and wagons in favor of motor trucks (which couldn't climb steep, muddy hills either). In December, 1910, the Marin Auto Livery Company was formed with service from Sausalito to Fort Baker using

a twenty-four-passenger motor bus. A seven-passenger touring car was planned for a livery service to meet all boats. John Teixeira, who with his brothers Manuel and Frank had operated a horse-drawn jitney service between Sausalito and Pine Station (Nevada Street), eventually switched to automobiles. The railroad ferries were forced by public demand to carry increasing numbers of automobiles, but still the railroad had not been significantly hurt. On one summer weekend in 1915, over 700 automobiles were ferried between San Francisco and Sausalito.

Around 1919, as the tide of automobiles became a flood, the railroad awakened to ominous signs of trouble ahead. One was a proposal of auto-bus service between Sausalito and San Rafael in direct competition with the Northwestern Pacific Railroad, with a promise of cheaper, faster service. Another was a proposal to start a second ferry service with boats designed to carry automobiles exclusively, from Fort Point on the San Francisco shore to Lime Point in Marin or possibly Sausalito. A third dark cloud for the railroad was a campaign by San Francisco and Marin newspapers urging construction of a highway bridge across the Golden Gate. In July, 1919, the Sausalito Board of Trustees unanimously endorsed the bridge proposal as a solution to Sausalito's auto congestion problem. The idea of spanning the Golden Gate went back as far as anyone could remember, though by 1919 it had become feasible in the minds of some and well within the limits of existing technology. But unlike the Brooklyn Bridge that linked one major metropolis with another, a Golden Gate bridge would link one city with a sprawling, undeveloped, and sparsely populated region. That fact made the bridge an idea whose time was slow in coming.

The bridge, however, was an attractive dream years away from realization; the automobile problem was a disagreeable reality. Long lines of waiting autos often stretched the length of Water Street as the ferryboats continued to give first priority to train passengers. Tempers flared, engines overheated, and horns honked as the boats maintained their strict timetables, disregarding the increased demand for auto transport.

In one such traffic jam in Sausalito, newspaperman Harry E. Speas missed the last boat to San Francisco one Sunday evening. Frustrated and angry, he determined to do something about the situation. In 1920 he incorporated the Golden Gate Ferry Company, dedicated to fast, efficient service for the motorist. Boats would run all night if need be, and extra boats would be pressed into service if demand warranted. Speas's problem was that he had no ferryboats, and stock sales were slower than expected. Speas approached Aven Hanford, president of the Rodeo-Vallejo Ferry Company, which had just launched a new auto ferry. Hanford and Oscar Klatt of the Rodeo-Vallejo

*A massive wooden platform was constructed by the Golden Gate Ferry Company. Here, c. 1926, autos leaving the ferry are heading north on Water Street. The Schnell building, center, is on the corner of Princess and Water Streets. The old Sausalito Land & Ferry Company sales office is on the right. Today the platform is gone, and Yee Tock Chee Park occupies part of the site.*

*Sausalito with two ferry terminals. The Golden Gate Ferry Company on the left, the Northwestern Pacific ferries on the right.*

With both ferry systems in operation during the 1920s, traffic jams became routine in Sausalito.
In 1926 Town Marshall Al O'Conner began giving tickets to automobiles parked over the sixty-minute
limit. Parking tickets were heralded by the Sausalito News as "the first step toward overcoming the
traffic congestion problem."

The electric sign on the right reads: "Keep to Right, Golden Gate Auto Ferry, Don't Turn Here." In this photo
looking south on Water Street from near the foot of San Carlos Avenue, fierce competition between the two
ferry systems is evident. Each tried to lure automobiles with flashing lights, uniformed traffic monitors, and
advertising campaigns. The building on the left is a railroad tower controlling the switches in the
Sausalito terminal.

*When the Northwestern Pacific Railroad felt threatened by the automobile, it not only built new ferryboats, but resorted to advertising its services in Sausalito for the first time.*

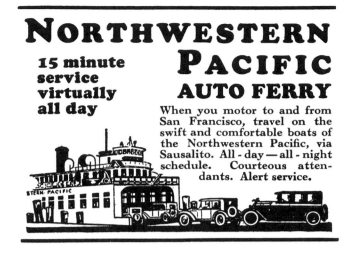

# NORTHWESTERN PACIFIC
## AUTO FERRY

**15 minute service virtually all day**

When you motor to and from San Francisco, travel on the swift and comfortable boats of the Northwestern Pacific, via Sausalito. All - day — all - night schedule. Courteous attendants. Alert service.

*The traffic problem became so severe by 1928 that "Marvelous Marin" offered to appoint a committee to study it. (right)*

line joined Speas as partners in the Golden Gate Ferry Company. General Manager and now vice-president Speas had no difficulty securing landing sites at the foot of Hyde Street in San Francisco and the foot of Princess Street in Sausalito. Ironically, the Sausalito landing slip was built on almost the same spot as the original ferryboat landing where the *Princess* began her career in 1868.

The Golden Gate Ferry Company inaugurated service on May 28, 1922, with the new *Aven J. Hanford,* on lease from the Rodeo-Vallejo Ferry Company. The first vessel designed expressly for the new run was the ferryboat *Golden Gate,* launched at Alameda in May, 1922; it was the world's first deisel-electric passenger ferry, fast and modern, with a capacity of eighty-five automobiles. The *Golden Gate* began ferrying autos on the 4th of July, 1922, and was an immediate hit with motorists.

The Northwestern Pacific Railroad, stung by slipping ferry revenues, was forced to compete with the Golden Gate Ferry Company. It enlarged and rebuilt the railroad car ferryboat *Ukiah* in 1923 to carry automobiles. She emerged from dry dock as the *Eureka,* largest ferryboat ever to operate on San Francisco Bay, with a capacity of 3,300 passengers and 100 automobiles. In another move to gain customers, the railroad planned three new steel ferryboats, each to carry ninety-five automobiles. However, these modern vessels, *Mendocino, Santa Rosa,* and *Redwood Empire,* did not go into service until 1927.

But all was not milk and honey for the fledgling Golden Gate Ferry Company. Praise soon turned to angry criticism as lines of autos waiting for the Golden Gate boats jammed the intersection of Princess and Water Street, adding to the traffic congestion rather than

relieving it. Speas promised more ferryboats would soon be in service. The *Golden West* was added in 1923, but the lines on weekends grew even longer. Uniformed traffic monitors were paid by the company to keep waiting autos in some semblance of order. The Northwestern Pacific Railroad complained that the traffic monitors, mistaken for policemen by motorists, were diverting customers from the NWP ferryboats to the Golden Gate landing. Residents complained that the downtown was no longer theirs. Rude drivers hurrying to the boats ignored pedestrians, and the lines of automobiles made it almost impossible for residents to use Water Street. The Sausalito Board of Trustees considered traffic lights at Princess Street and El Portal as a solution. The *Sausalito News* recommended pedestrian bridges over Water Street at key locations. The Golden Gate Ferry Company added a second ferry slip in 1926, with the promise of faster service. But still the cars came. On the July 10th weekend in 1926, the combined Golden Gate and Northwestern Pacific ferries carried over 70,000 automobiles.

The public had grown impatient with the railroad and the ferryboats, both developed to meet the needs of an earlier era. The automobile now symbolized an intoxicating personal independence from the old forms of public transportation. Marin residents turned on the railroad that had served them for decades, bitterly criticizing the outdated railway cars, the slow schedules, dilapidated and unsafe platforms and stations, and the cumbersome ferryboats. The railroad, they claimed, had failed to keep pace with the needs of a changing Marin County. Local commuters in their impatience were experiencing symptoms of an upheaval rapidly becoming worldwide—the

*The NWP ferryboats up until 1927 were all designed in the preautomobile era.*

birth pangs of what Aldous Huxley in 1932 was to call the Brave New World, born on the date of the invention of the Model T. Naturally enough, what frustrated the people trying to get to San Francisco as fast as possible was the local, present traffic jam. At best the two ferryboat systems could transport 1,000 autos an hour. But it was not enough.

The competing ferryboat systems were merged in 1929, when Southern Pacific, parent company of the Northwestern Pacific Railroad, bought out the seven-year-old Golden Gate Ferry Company and created a new company called Southern Pacific-Golden Gate Ferries Ltd. The company had a total of twenty-seven boats serving Oakland, San Francisco, Alameda, Berkeley, and Sausalito. On Sunday nights when peak traffic was returning to San Francisco from Sausalito, the new company could divert boats from other runs to Sausalito. Ferryboats loaded with autos left Sausalito's Golden Gate ferry slip every twelve minutes. But in the motoring public's opinion that was still not enough.

However, also in 1929, the Golden Gate Bridge District was organized, after officially incorporating on December 4, 1928. Its principal business was to build a bridge. The last link in the Redwood Highway would soon be forged, ending Sausalito's ferryboat era.

*A ferryboat man if ever there was one: Sausalitan Per Anderson in 1925 as a deckhand for the Northwestern Pacific Railroad.*

*The crew of the ferryboat* Sausalito *and some friends, c. 1927. On the far left is Jimmy Martoni; fourth from left, Sausalito police officer James Doyle; next to him is First Mate Rudy Petterson. The two concession stand ladies are Margaret Johnson and Mary Bass.*

*A small parade, occasion unrecorded, passed through Water Street in 1924. Mason's Garage, built in 1924 to accommodate commuters' automobiles, looms behind the marchers.*

133

*The Stephen Brigante family about to launch a new fishing boat at his Atlantic Boat Building Plant, c. 1910.*

$B$oatbuilding in Sausalito has been a continuing activity from William Richardson's time to the present. The Cove in Old Town provided an ideal site for the construction and repair of boats. The flat, protected beach and plentiful supply of wood and water were noted by the earliest observers. Richardson worked on his boats there in the 1840s, and probably John Reed before him also took advantage of the Cove's natural amenities. It is very possible that the U.S. Navy built launching ways there in the early 1850s before the Mare Island dry dock was in operation.

Photographs of the 1880s show fishing feluccas in the Cove and elsewhere along Sausalito's waterfront, when boatbuilding was mainly a family affair, each building boats for personal use. By 1890 the California Launch Building Company was established near the foot of Richardson Street in Old Town. Superintendent Lanteri reported the launch of a large tugboat and an eighty-five-foot steamer that year. Brixen and Munfrey's Boatyard was in the Cove around 1900, and the Reliance Boat and Ways Company was located there in the 1920s, turning out yachts, launches, and barges.

The best-known boatbuilders in Old Town were the Nunes Brothers Boat and Ways Company, established in 1925. Manuel and Antonio Nunes came from the Azores

*The dock and marine ways at Nunes Brothers boatyard in the Cove, c. 1940. The old Spreckels boathouse is in the background, and four new Mercury kit boats, designed by Ernie Nunes, are on the dock.*

*The graceful 127-foot schooner* Zaca, *built by the Nunes Brothers was launched in 1930. Commissioned by banker Templeton Crocker,* Zaca *was taken on a cruise around the world shortly after launching; no expense was spared in her construction. She carried a crew of eighteen including a doctor and Crocker's valet. During the 1930s* Zaca *made scientific voyages returning with exotic flora and fauna. After World War II and service as a coastal patrol boat,* Zaca *was sold to actor Errol Flynn who used her to the fullest in his pursuit of pleasure. Reportedly she is still afloat in a French port, dismasted and in disrepair.*

Amiga Mia, *a sixty-five-foot twin screw diesel cruiser built by Nunes Brothers, starts down the ways September 20, 1929. Owner Edwin Merry stands on the foredeck while his son William Merry in white trousers crouches on the foredeck and H. R. Rieschel is barely visible behind the fluttering jack. Little Barbara Tullis has just sent a bottle of sparkling burgundy toward* Amiga Mia's *bow as a crowd of over 100 workers, salmon fishermen, boatmen, and friends watch the event.*

*In 1928 Nunes Brothers Boat and Ways Company built the* Funchal *and* Greyhound, *two 112-foot tuna clippers. They are shown here under construction on the Nunes ways at the foot of Main Street with the* Walhalla *in the background.*

*The crew and friends at Madden and Lewis Company, Boat Builders and Marine Ways, at the foot of Locust Street, c. 1943. The Madden and Lewis boatyard, which suffered two disastrous fires, in 1920 and in 1964, was a happier scene on this day. All the names are not recorded, but the group includes Dick Lewis; Matts and Toots Perry; Joe, Al, Frank, and Menotti Pasquinucci; Myron Spaulding; Ray Bottarini; Sil Tenconi; Harry Gallagher; Ralph Flowers; Lorraine Rocha; Andy Bettencourt; and George Ennis. Nick Cordelia; Manuel Peters; Mrs. A. L. Lewis; Rodney McDermott; Adele Pasquinucci Tenconi; Wesley Church; Kathryn Madden Bassford; Frank Olivera; and Manuel Mancebo.*

in the 1890s and had been boatbuilders on the Sacramento River and in Oakland constructing tugboats, barges, and other utilitarian craft. In Sausalito they took over the Reliance Boat and Ways Company at Second and Main Streets and for the next thirty-five years Nunes Brothers produced a variety of power and sailing vessels, including successful racing boats.

The beaches of New Town also saw small-scale boat-building in the 1880s. Later the Oceanic Boatyard and Stephen Brigante's Atlantic Boat Building Works were established there. Menotti Pasquinucci, Madden and Lewis, and C. H. Arques are names that became familiar to

Sausalitans by the 1920s. During World War II, the local boatyards did their part. Madden and Lewis built motor launches for the Royal Navy, harbor towboats, and 110-foot torpedo patrol boats for the U.S. Navy. Arques built barges and lighters, and Nunes Brothers constructed tugs. The Oakland Shipbuilding Company built a yard north of Napa Street to fulfill government contracts for barges. The name was changed to the Sausalito Shipbuilding Company during the war and the marine ways were enlarged to handle large fishing boats with an eye toward postwar business. This yard eventually became known as Bob's Boatyard.

Sausalitans have always taken two contradictory attitudes toward their town. They listen enthusiastically to optimistic promoters of new ideas for expansion and increased prosperity. But they are equally receptive to voices that caution against change and advocate protection of Sausalito as it is. Like most small-town citizens, Sausalitans in the past have been small-town boosters, hoping to see their town grow. In the 1880s and 1890s, the lure to attract new residents was cheap land and pure water. In the 1920s it was the easy commute to San Francisco and the promise of fast profits once the Golden Gate Bridge was built and the Redwood Empire opened to development. In the 1930s, depression years, some Sausalitans were game to listen to any scheme that might provide jobs and possibly trigger a new boom.

But there is a contrary side to the collective character of the townspeople, a side that loves the tranquil beauty and smallness of Sausalito and fiercely opposes anything perceived as injurious to those qualities. These opposite attitudes of enthusiasm for (on the one hand) and rejection of (on the other) change exist at the same time in the body politic of the town. Developers sometimes find these traits irreconcilable.

An example of such conflict occurred in 1930, when Oakland boatbuilders W. F. Stone & Son proposed relocating in Sausalito's cove, next to Nunes Brothers' boatyard. The news was instantly hailed as a boon to Sausalito's depression economy. Stone & Son, in business since 1854, were highly respected as builders of some of the finest boats on the Bay. As hearings progressed, however, uncertainty over the proposal was growing. What about noise? And the unsightly buildings? Maybe the boatyard should be located at the north end of town. The final blow was dealt by Sausalito's elite of the elite, William Randolph Hearst. He was so elite he didn't even live in Sausalito. But, as he reminded everyone through his "Piedmont Land & Cattle Company," he was one of the largest property owners in Sausalito. His benevolence included keeping a close eye on the town's development. The Stone & Son Boatyard would be, in his opinion, an unwarranted industrial intrusion into an otherwise residential community. Three weeks later the Sausalito Trustees voted down the boatyard proposal. Yielding to pressure? Perhaps.

But there has always been a split personality at work in Sausalito, a "Jekyll and Hyde" personality according to some developers. This attitude is easily recognized in local newspaper editorials of the 1920s and 1930s. For example, the launch of the magnificent yacht *Zaca* by Nunes Brothers in 1929 brought praise from the citizenry and applause to Templeton Crocker for having the good sense to spend his money in Sausalito to build *Zaca*. Then several weeks after the launching, an editorial attacked Crocker for letting a gasoline-powered generator run past midnight on *Zaca* as she was anchored in the cove, disturbing the sleep of nearby residents.

This attitude of "we want to have our cake and eat it too" has always disturbed Sausalito's sister cities in Marin and around the bay; Sausalito has a reputation as a difficult place in which to promote development. But Sausalito residents take this criticism in stride, their positive feelings for the town easily outweighing the criticism. Everyone who lives in Sausalito or has lived there, except for those born there, remembers the first time he saw Sausalito. For many it was love at first sight. Early Portuguese settlers thought it was like the Azores. The British were reminded of the small coves and inlets of Devonshire or Cornwall. Many early San Franciscans thought of Sausalito as a refuge. After the initial discovery, Sausalito either lives up to one's expectations or it does not, in which case one leaves. For those who stay, the town gets in the blood and newcomers become old-timers and staunch defenders of Sausalito.

Sausalito with its mix of cultures and people has never been a melting pot. It has never been a smooth broth, either, but rather a lumpy chowder with gritty bits in it. It is a small town without a small town's singleness of purpose. The long-ago vision of Sausalito as a sister metropolis to San Francisco has vanished. The notion in the last century that Sausalito would one day *be* something — Navy base, industrial center, transportation hub — led residents to promote and to resist those goals at the same time. In doing so, they inadvertently gave Sausalito her true character and made the town what it is today.

People are drawn to Sausalito today because of the character of the town that has been created by its residents. The founders of Sausalito might not see the citizens of today as inheritors of their town, but if they sat through a City Council meeting they would be quick to recognize them.

---

The vision of Richardon's Bay as a navy base was a popular and persistent one. Emerging in the 1920s was a more novel idea: Richardson Bay as a great flying-boat base. After Lindbergh's trans-Atlantic solo flight, aviation caught the nation's fancy as never before. Aircraft manufacturer Anthony Fokker visited Marin in 1927, praising the county as a natural site for the aircraft industry. The Marine Aircraft Company was formed in Sausalito in 1930 to produce small seaplanes. The prototype, *Water Sprite* was not yet completed when the firm was reorganized as the Triton Aircraft Company, with offices at Caledonia and Pine and assembly plant at the foot of Napa Street. In 1931 after two successful test flights, the four-place, pale green biplane had its portrait taken at Napa Street. Soon after, Sausalito's only airplance manufacturer and its sole output, the *Water Sprite* flew off into the misty skies of history and were heard from no more.

Water Sprite, *later renamed* Triton *(right) built by the Triton Aircraft Company of Sausalito. Left to right: Charles Richter; Phil Solerman, designer; Henry Jones; Edward Cuppage, general manager; and Guy Turner, chief mechanic.*

---

*Water Street at the plaza* c. 1929. *Sausalito on the eve of the Depression had the look of a prosperous, bustling little community. The trio on the corner could be discussing the latest innovation at the Princess Theater, talking pictures.*

In spite of agreement on many issues, Sausalitans have traditionally split along one predictable line: that between the Hill and the Waterfront. In the 1870s the distinction formed naturally. Wealthy Americans and upper-class Europeans built on the choice-view lots and commuted to offices in San Francisco. Their servants, plus tradesmen, local merchants, and craftsmen settled on the waterfront in modest homes. Here they lived and worked, either on the water or on what little flat land Sausalito had. The influx of gamblers and saloon habitués in the 1890s gave the waterfront an unsavory reputation that lasted for over two decades. "Hillclimbers" and "Water Rats" were at odds on many issues. Ironically, the automobile brought them closer together. The affordable automobiles of the 1920s made almost everyone middle class, all seeking the same goals, such as better streets and safer traffic controls. Differences of opinion have not altogether disappeared, however, and won't in the future. But Sausalitans do have in common a love for the town and a strong sense of civic-mindedness.

If the focus of the 1920s was on homebuilding and road improvements in Sausalito, the 1930s was a time of declining fortunes and rising expectations. The confident real-estate market came to an end after the stock market collapse of 1929. Editorials in the local newspaper, once boasting of the certain boom soon to engulf Sausalito, gave way to cautious optimism and a rallying call to "Buy in Sausalito." Then the long-awaited start of construction on the Golden Gate Bridge boosted spirits as well as provided construction jobs.

By 1932, grand development plans once more emerged in Sausalito. Albert von der Werth, representing the Golden Gate Yacht Harbor, Ltd., proposed converting dormant Shelter Cove into a 300-berth yacht marina that would not only incorporate within its bounds Nunes Brothers' boatyard, but also have facilities for commercial fishing. The project thus qualified for funding by President Roosevelt's Public Works Administration. The proposal dragged on through many months of negotiation with Washington and finally failed for lack of matching funds. On that project and on the proposed "lateral," or second, highway north from the Golden Gate through Sausalito were pinned the hopes of many residents and merchants. If such an enormous project as the Golden Gate Bridge could be undertaken in the depths of the Depression, then perhaps there was hope for Sausalito yet. Perhaps one needed to look beyond the confines of Sausalito . . . to all of Richardson's Bay.

Richardson's Bay, the broad, shallow body of water that is Sausalito's front yard, has always been a source of inspiration and the object of fantasies for speculators. Its potential for development has spawned countless schemes from the reasonable to the absurd. Even Joseph Strauss, chief engineer for the Golden Gate Bridge, could not resist venturing an opinion on what ought to be done with that big, empty bay. In December, 1935, almost midway in construction on the bridge, Strauss unveiled his plan. Stating bluntly that Sausalito and adjacent towns offered nothing to tourists, he proposed filling the upper half of

Richardson's Bay to create a site for an amusement park on Strawberry Point, an airfield, an athletic field, coliseum and stadium, and perhaps a zoo. Sausalito would be the gateway to this visitors' delight via the "lateral" highway. Never a timid thinker, Strauss suggested financing by the federal government to reclaim this "almost worthless" waterway wherein the Navy could locate an aviation training school.

In an age of bold projects and a prevailing "can do" attitude, Strauss's plan drew favorable response from Congressman Clarence Lea and Marin County planners, who were then, as now, pondering the fate of Richardson's Bay. Sausalito officials particularly liked the part that called for filling in the Sausalito shoreline out to the bulkhead line, about 500 yards beyond today's shoreline. This would be an industrial site, where "rail and ocean commerce would meet." Strauss's plan, in his words, would fit "into the general scheme of making Marvelous Marin the playground for the San Francisco Bay area."

The most ambitious plan for Richardson's Bay had been formulated in 1912, when local boosters persuaded the federal government to survey the hills west of Sausalito for a ship canal into the bay from the Pacific Ocean. A four-mile cut was planned through a gap in the rolling hills at the head of Tennessee Cove, up Elk Valley to the bay south of Dolan's Corner in Mill Valley. Engineers were basking in the glory of the Panama Canal achievement and doubtless saw opportunities for construction marvels everywhere. If Panama could have a canal, so could Sausalito.

The ship-canal plan was resurrected in 1936 when Richardson's Bay was being promoted as the logical site for a submarine base for the Navy. A Pacific opening to Richardson's Bay would eliminate the need for dredging and provide for ships a fog-free entrance to San Francisco Bay that would by-pass Potato Patch shoals. If Stockton could have a deep-water port, so could Sausalito.

The idea of making Richardson's Bay into a submarine base first came up in 1933 when the Navy announced it might be looking for a West Coast site. The Sausalito City Council had long been seeking a dredged ship-channel along the Sausalito shoreline to Waldo Point to generate business for waterfront property. If the Navy took over the bay, it was reasoned, Sausalito would have her channel plus a thriving business with the Navy. If Vallejo could have a Navy base, why not Sausalito?

Sausalito's submarine base plan fell on deaf ears in Washington, and in 1937 even the request for dredging the ship channel was rejected by the War Department as being strictly a "local project" without merit for national defense. That same year, however, the War Department saw Richardson's Bay in another light. With the increasing threat of war, Washington proposed reserving the bay for seaplanes, with an anchorage for seaplane tenders, destroyers, and other light vessels. That plan, too, died aborning. And it wasn't until war was declared and Sausalito's shipyard was under construction in 1942 that the long-awaited ship channel was dredged in Richardson's Bay. Since World War II the channel has been kept cleared

© 1930
ters & Hainlin Studios
Oakland, Calif.

of silt by the Army Corps of Engineers as part of its bay maintenance program.

Richardson's Bay was touted as the logical site for the 1939 World's Fair. When the fair was over, it was argued an airport could be built on bay fill that would complement the existing railroad terminus and ferryboat system, making Sausalito a major transportation hub. The selected site, however, was Goat Island shoals, which was filled and became Treasure Island.

Much of the motivation for development schemes in the 1930s was an honest effort to create local jobs to ease the burden of the deep economic depression. The stirring sight of two colossal bridges (the Oakland Bay Bridge and the Golden Gate Bridge) under construction simultaneously stimulated planners and speculators alike. Sausalito was not alone in wanting an end to unemployment and despair. It came . . . on December 7, 1941.

*Sausalito in 1930, looking east from Wolfback Ridge. New Town is on the left, the Hill in the middle, and Old Town on the right. This looks like a contemporary photograph, but there are differences. Both ferry systems are in operation. The ferryboat* Cazadero *is in the NWPRR slip with the little* Marin *alongside the wharf. In the Golden Gate Ferry Company slips near the foot of Princess Street are two vessels, either the* San Mateo, Shasta, *or* Yosemite. Richardson's Bay *still has a few large sailing ships at anchor, and the main activity on Belvedere is the Union Codfish Company plant on the shoreline which burned in 1937. Tiburon in 1930 was little more than railroad yards and shops and the ferry landing. On Sausalito's "hogsback," in the left foreground, there are a few homes but mainly grass. It was here in 1919 that the Old Town fire began. A fire originating here in 1933 would again threaten Old Town with prevailing winds carrying the blaze across Prospect Avenue and Sausalito Boulevard in several places.*

*In this 1927 photo, Augie Perry (Mrs. Fred Perry) stands in front of Budworth's with Mr. Nelson on the right. The small boy on his tricycle is unidentified, but he probably lives around Caledonia Street today and will recognize himself.*

*Small businesses in Sausalito during the Depression struggled for survival, but most made it. In 1927 Mrs. C. W. Budworth purchased the school supply and candy store at Locust and Caledonia Streets from Manuel Beirao. The year 1929 brought not only the stock market crash but also the death of her husband. Mrs. Budworth and her two daughters persevered, however, and the shop continued under their proprietorship until it was closed in 1977.*

In the 1930s the trend to put the waterfront to more productive use continued. Arks, like the one above owned by Mr. and Mrs. Merle Akers, were moved or demolished. Rather than lose their investment, the Akers had their ark moved from the foot of Napa Street, shown here with Caledonia Street in the foreground, looking north. The structure was winched up to a new foundation on Hannon's Hill where it remains today. In 1933 the Sausalito Board of Trustees ordered the removal of numerous hulks that were abandoned in Richardson's Bay near the Sausalito shoreline.

*There were many morale-boosting events and activities (left) in Sausalito during the Depression. On Memorial Day, 1934, a memorial to Sausalito servicemen killed in World War I was dedicated in front of the plaza fountain. The Veterans of Foreign Wars and the Ladies Auxiliary, Daniel F. Madden Post, placed a time capsule beneath the concrete obelisk. In 1977, as part of a restoration project, the monument was moved to the north end of the plaza and rededicated to the dead of all wars and a new time capsule was deposited beneath it.*

*Decorated for a parade in 1933, the Holly Oaks Hotel's official automobile carries a declaration of support for Franklin Roosevelt's National Recovery Act.*

143

*Interior of Red Gables on Spencer Avenue c. 1932. Not everyone suffered during the Depression. This stylish living room is a graphic example of the good life in hard times.*

*Villa Ladera on Bulkley Avenue was the home of Lorenzo Scatena, who died one month after its completion in 1930. Built on the site of his former home, the $75,000 mansion was the realization of Scatena's dream to recreate a memory of his childhood in Lucca, Italy. A Sausalito resident since 1910, Scatena came to this country in 1862 at age twelve to live with his uncle, a farmer in Half Moon Bay. In 1877 he met Mrs. Virginia Giannini, a young widow with three sons. After going into business for himself he married her and moved to San Francisco. After a successful career in real estate, Scatena and his sons started the Italian Bank of California, which soon became the Bank of Italy. He was president until 1915 when his son, Amadeo P. Giannini took over, and Scatena became chairman of the board. Shortly after Scatena's death, the bank became Bank of America.*

144

*View from the Alta Mira Hotel c. 1930. Sausalito hotels, for decades the symbol of gracious living, were forced to reduce rates and services during the Depression. A room at the Sausalito Hotel on El Portal went for eighteen dollars a month in 1933, or twenty-two dollars a month with private bath.*

The new Alta Mira Hotel was opened in September, 1927, amid much fanfare. It was built on the site of the original Alta Mira, once the private residence of Thomas W. "Tapeworm" Jackson and his wife in the 1880s. Jackson converted this villa into a hotel in 1895, keeping the name Alta Mira. By the 1920s the management claimed that the famous hostelry had housed over one-third of all the people living in Sausalito. On December 23, 1926, the hotel burned to the ground. Heroic efforts by the Sausalito Fire Department saved not only the surrounding hillside homes but also the small cottages on the hotel grounds. Thomas Jackson's son Ernest rebuilt the Alta Mira as a Spanish-style villa that quickly caught the fancy of Sausalitans and their guests.

*Some people made ends meet by working at second jobs, or "moonlighting." Russ Bacon, a Sausalito jeweler, ran a taxi service in the early 1930s between Sausalito and the forts. Army officers were good customers with steady jobs and cash on hand.*

*The Challenge: build a bridge across the Golden Gate, from Fort Point on the San Francisco shore (foreground) to Lime Point in the Marin headlands c. 1930.*

Construction of the Golden Gate Bridge and the San Francisco-Oakland Bay Bridge during the Depression was a symbol of hope. The national economy was in shambles, but work on the bridges continued, inspiring those who watched the colossal towers rise day-by-day from the bay waters. The $35,000,000 bond issue to build the Golden Gate Bridge had been approved by voters on November 4, 1930, just short of a year after the stock market crash. The vote climaxed a hard, eleven-year struggle that began when Joseph P. Strauss, who would eventually build the bridge, met with San Francisco city engineer O'Shaunessy and was convinced that the bridge was feasible.

Sausalitans, for the most part, supported the plan to build a bridge. Completing the last link in the Redwood Highway would not only end traffic congestion in Sausalito, but boost the economy of Marin County. The boom that would put Sausalito on the map, anticipated for over a generation, would surely come when a bridge to San Francisco was built. In a 1926 editorial, the *Sausalito News* expressed confidence in Sausalito's future: "If you hold business property on or near the Redwood Highway, hold on to it. Buy more. Prosperity and increase in value are headed this way. The Redwood Highway will become one of the most famous highways of the world. A

nation a-wheel will pass this way. And with a Golden Gate Bridge at one end of this road, the world would flock to our front yard." The local newspaper even went so far as to predict a boom equivalent to that occurring in Los Angeles at the time: "Prominent local real estate men are confident that the coming spring will see much Sausalito property turned, and at high prices. A walk or ride through any section of Sausalito will reveal the number of new houses, garages and new buildings. In time to come this city will be built back many miles, into what is now hill land considered good only for cow pasture. Those who own this acreage will become wealthy sub-division plutocrats after the manner of some Hollywood folks. A little of the right kind of advertising and promotion will hasten the day of this prosperity."

Of particular interest to Sausalito was early consideration by the bridge planners of a primary approach to the bridge through Sausalito. A water-level approach had considerable merit but was rejected when costs for property condemnation were projected. It was decided that the main approach would be a long, direct highway up from Waldo Point, to be known as the Waldo Grade. This route had some disadvantages: huge cuts through rock would have to be made, and the hilly area was subject to dense fog and high winds and landslides. For these reasons, a second approach, or "lateral," would be necessary. The Redwood Highway would have a by-pass through Sausalito, and a new road would be cut through Fort Baker connecting with the Golden Gate Bridge. Sausalito would be linked to the bridge after all.

As the propoganda wars were being waged over the Golden Gate Bridge, the main activity of bridge planners in the 1920s was in the courtroom. Litigation brought by individuals and groups opposed to the bridge dragged on for years. After the California legislature passed the Golden Gate Bridge Highway Act in 1923 that authorized creation of a special bridge district with power to levy taxes, the legal battle began. Joseph Strauss, still an unpaid engineering consultant, refuted the arguments that a Golden Gate span would be unsafe. Sausalito attorney George H. Harlan, also an unpaid consultant, successfully battled in the courts on behalf of the bridge. At last, on December 4, 1928, the Golden Gate Bridge District was incorporated. Incorporation led to a new wave of litigation.

The propaganda campaign supporting a bridge over the Golden Gate took a vicious turn after it was revealed that Southern Pacific-Golden Gate Ferries, Ltd., was party to a lawsuit attempting to block the bridge project. Southern Pacific warned that a bridge would be an enormous cost to taxpayers. The *Sausalito News* hired well-known landscape painter and Sausalitan Maynard Dixon to draw editorial cartoons depicting Southern Pacific as a villain. In one rather heavy-handed drawing, Dixon shows the inevitable fate of commuters if the bridge is not built. The ferryboats, with an outstanding safety record over fifty-five years of service, are depicted as floating deathtraps.

Not all Sausalito residents were pleased by the prospect of what the Golden Gate Bridge might bring. Some were content to see the swarms of weekend visitors pass right through, fearing what might happen to Sausalito if it were "discovered." Mabel K. Eastman wrote in 1927 her view of "the only undiscovered suburb of San Francisco."

"Sausalito: Where morals are easy and suppressed emotions find expression; where matrimonial bonds grow loose and sometimes slip off; where every other person you meet is either famous or notorious; the only waterfront in this vicinity that smells like fresh clams and not like mud flats. To the majority in San Francisco or anywhere, Sausalito is just some place to go through . . . the entrance to beautiful Marin. And we, sitting on the hill, hold tight for fear they will find us. The day we are discovered we are lost. So this is not a complaint — it's an exclamation. Residents can remain undisturbed so long as the crowds go through. And Heaven keep them going through! It's Sausalito's salvation."

But the majority of Sausalito's 3,000 residents in the late 1920s sympathized with "Marvelous Marin," a countywide boosters' club incorporated in 1927 to promote the bridge and publicize the wonders of Marin County. Editors of the *Sausalito News* expressed the popular sentiment of the time: "Let's help San Francisco to discover Sausalito. Sausalito is the most accessible of any residential suburb to the city of San Francisco. . . . It is the cream suburb of the Bay region. It is time to tell the world about Sausalito."

---

*A* Sausalito News *editorial, October 24, 1930, carried under Maynard Dixon's drawing when Southern Pacific-Golden Gate Ferries, Ltd., opposed construction of the Golden Gate Bridge.*

"Look, ye who cringe when the transportation giant speaks! Look, ye — and remember!
When the transportation giant cracks his whip there are puppets who scuttle to do his bidding — to prostitute their heritage of manhood.

"The transportation giant and his puppets would hide the fact that under the present system LIVES and not Gold will be forfeit that the people may be called upon to pay. SOME DAY — THE FOG — —!

"Just four words, but what tragedy they spell. Until now the fathers and mothers crossing the bay each day have been fortunate. Only occasionally have there been sorrowing dependents left at home. SOME DAY — THE FOG — —!

"If the transportation giant and his puppets have their way that day might be expected. Until now a kindly Providence has protected against the horror pictured above.
But, ye who cringe when the transportation giant speaks — Look, ye and remember —
SOME DAY — THE FOG — —!"

147

While the Golden Gate Bridge project was stalled, other men with dreams of bridges were busily at work. A proposal for a span between San Francisco and Oakland was revived after an earlier proposal was rejected by the War Department which feared that a bridge would block movement of warships in the bay. In 1928 T. A. Tomasini planned a toll bridge from Albany in the East Bay to Bluff Point near Tiburon in Marin County. In that same year, Charles Van Damme, president of the Richmond San Rafael Bridge Company, proposed a bridge from Richmond to San Rafael to replace his auto ferryboats. Tomasini then proposed a toll drawbridge across Richardson's Bay from the foot of Napa Street in Sausalito to the northern tip of Belvedere, a bridge that would benefit Sausalito and particularly Tiburon by opening the Tiburon peninsula for development. By the end of 1928, Tomasini, with an Army Engineer's permit for his Sausalito-Belvedere bridge, began drilling test bores in the bay floor just off Napa Street. The coincidental merger of the Golden Gate Ferry Company with the Northwestern Pacific ferry service caused second thoughts in Belvedere and Tiburon about Tomasini's project.

Fearing the potential loss of direct ferry service to San Francisco and possibly even railroad service if the bridge were built, Belvedere withdrew consent for the project. The Depression put a damper on Tomasini's other bridge proposals, and none of them ever came to fruition.

On January 5, 1933, construction began on the Golden Gate Bridge when steam shovels chewed into Lime Point where the Marin anchorage would be. An official groundbreaking ceremony in February raised hopes of Sausalito residents that prosperity might indeed be just around the corner. Sausalito's contribution to the construction of the Golden Gate Bridge over the next four years was small compared to the enormity of the project. Yet each participant felt a part of the historic project. Sausalito's Rudy Petterson was engaged in various construction activities from the first test borings to the last rivets, mainly as a barge captain and rigging foreman. Boatbuilders Madden and Lewis were contracted to build the huge cofferdam surrounding the Marin tower foundation. Many other Sausalitans found work on the project at various stages of construction, although the large contractors usually brought their own work force.

In September, 1933, a Sausalito Lions Club committee consisting of Henry Meyer, Frank B. Anderson (publisher of the *Sausalito News*), Robert Miller, and Ernest W. Jackson presented a "rapid transit" highway scheme to the Bridge District. The plan again called for the main highway to the Golden Gate Bridge to run through Sausalito rather than over the Waldo Grade. An eighty-foot-high elevated freeway would enter Sausalito from the south at Alexander Avenue, traverse Shelter Cove outboard of land, and reach ground level near the Golden Gate Ferry

*Lime Point in 1933 with Needle Rock to the left, looking across to San Francisco. Preliminary work has commenced on the Marin anchorage of the Golden Gate Bridge.*

One of the grooved cable saddles on the Marin tower, 690 feet above the foundation pier.

Pacific Railroad freight station near the foot of Johnson Street would have to be moved to make way for the new highway. When it was relocated on the vacant lot below Central School, residents who now had to look down on it complained. They suggested that a new stucco facade and a red tile "Spanish style" roof would make the shed more attractive. Railroad workers painted the roof red as a compromise.

Caledonia Street merchants were not excited about the main street through New Town being rerouted. They were assured, however, that it was to their benefit. Motorists hurrying to and from the ferryboats were seldom customers; they just made Caledonia Street dangerous for pedestrians. With a new highway outboard of Caledonia near the NWP tracks, Caledonia Street would become a comfortable, resident-serving street. Property owners who faced condemnation proceedings on their trackside parcels were harder to placate. It took over a year of legal wrangling before all were satisfied.

landing. An underpass would be located at the Northwestern Pacific ferry terminal to accommodate commuters. From there the modern highway would continue through Sausalito to Waldo Point. Reaction from Bridge District officials was quick. No change from the approved Waldo Grade plan would be contemplated. Sausalito would be linked to the bridge as planned, via a two-lane lateral to be constructed as a Public Works Administration project. But the prospect of a major highway cutting through Sausalito never died away. It surfaced again in 1946 when traffic over the Golden Gate span warranted expanded freeway access.

As work on the bridge continued, Sausalito went about its business, which was slow. There was so little home building activity that the *Sausalito News* commented: "Most papers boost their towns by telling about all the building permits taken out during the past twelve months. Building permits here are a lot of blah, so why mention them?"

But little changes were taking place, important to a few, unnoticed by many. The last of Sausalito's "pioneers" passed from the scene in the 1930s. Even the second generation of merchants and residents was yielding to the passage of time. Fred Fiedler, the Water Street grocer whose father had started the business in 1885, retired, and the grocery was converted to a "5¢ to 25¢" store. The ferryboat *Marin,* long an institution on Richardson's Bay, made her last run from Sausalito to Tiburon on December 21, 1933. The aging little vessel had carried a generation of commuters between the two communities. She was replaced by Greyhound buses. In 1933 the California Highway Commission announced that the Redwood Highway would be extended into Sausalito, with a new road from Napa Street south to the intersection of Water Street and San Carlos Avenue. The old Northwestern

*Previously unpublished photographs of Golden Gate Bridge construction taken by Sausalito photographer Dulce Duncan in 1934. Here, a diver prepares to descend during work on the San Francisco pier.*

*Work on the San Francisco pier continues as the Marin tower nears completion.*

When the new state highway from Nevada Street south to San Carlos was under construction in 1935, Sausalito's postmaster Robert Frost asked the City Council what the name of the new street was to be. A discussion led to the proposal by postmaster Frost that whatever the name, it should apply to the entire length of Sausalito to avoid confusion on mailboxes. A five-dollar prize was offered for the best name for Sausalito's new street. A year later when the new section of highway was complete, few names had been submitted. The best of these were Portal del Norte, Rolph Way, Golden Gate Boulevard, and Frost's suggestion, Bridgeway Boulevard. Councilman Rudy Petterson recommended Bridgeway as the most appropriate. The prize was withdrawn due to lack of interest, and a motion was made and unanimously approved to drop Water Street in favor of Bridgeway Boulevard all the way from the northern city limit to Richardson Street. Mayor Herb Madden said that Bridgeway "sounded like 'the way to the bridge' and that motorists will be more likely to drive into town rather than take the mainline approach."

As of July 7, 1936, reported the *Sausalito News,* "Water Street, symbolic of a lower stratum in Sausalito's social life, quite uncouth for such an aesthetic community, is no more." By 1938 Bridgeway Boulevard seemed a bit pretentious for such a small town, and the name was changed again, simply to Bridgeway.

Another minor event occurred in 1935 that marked the passing of Sausalito's early days. The town became a city. A petition changing Sausalito's status from a town to a sixth-class California city was circulated and signed by over twenty-five percent of the registered voters. The Board of Trustees became the City Council, and the Town Marshall, the Chief of Police.

In 1936 as Sausalito waited out the Depression, work continued on the four-lane Waldo Grade approach to the Golden Gate Bridge. Sausalitans watched with fascination as the Waldo Tunnel was blasted through the hill beneath Appetite Rock, and bulldozers carved the new highway along Sausalito's western edge. As the bridge neared completion, discussion turned to the fate of the ferryboats. Some assumed that there would be sufficient business for both bridge and ferries, although it was generally conceded that service to Hyde Street in San Francisco would be dropped. The Northwestern Pacific Railroad claimed in 1936 that it was losing $200,000 a year on interurban service and wanted to abandon its commuter trains. The equipment, it claimed, was worn out, and

*Randolph Nicolai Petterson, better known as Rudy Petterson, c. 1912, was a bridge worker, but not a typical one. Petterson was born in Norway in 1887 and went to sea at age fifteen. He settled in Sausalito as a master seaman in 1914, and the next year at the Panama Pacific International Exposition he won the amateur light-heavyweight boxing championship. He became a master ship rigger, served in the U.S. Revenue Service, and was first mate and pilot on the NWPRR Ferryboats. As a captain for the Golden Gate Ferry Company, Petterson also held the candy and cigar franchise on all the Golden Gate boats. He started work on the Golden Gate Bridge project in 1929 as a barge foreman and rigger and worked on different phases of bridge construction until opening day in 1937. He also served fifteen years on the Sausalito City Council and two years as a Marin County Supervisor.*

with competition from the soon-to-open Golden Gate Bridge, there was little justification to put money in the system. The electric railcars were mostly wooden ones dating back twenty-eight to thirty-five years, and the NWP ferryboats were mainly an aging fleet. The handwriting was on the wall. The age of interurban rail transit in Marin County was rapidly coming to a close.

After an awkward ceremony on April 28, 1937, during which ironworkers Edward Murphy and Edward Stanley crushed a symbolic gold rivet into a hole at midspan, the Golden Gate Bridge was officially opened to traffic on May 28, 1937, amid much hoopla. The previous day had been Pedestrian Day, when 200,000 people crossed the span on foot. Within days of the opening came complaints from residents in Old Town about the incessant horn-honking in the Waldo Tunnel as motorists expressed their enthusiasm for the new wonder of the age. That same week, the Ferry Garage on Bridgeway closed down as customers vanished.

With the opening of the Golden Gate Bridge, Sausalito became totally committed to the automobile, not only as the principal means of ingress and egress, but as the prime mover of change. Now that Sausalito had a through highway and was no longer a cul-de-sac, the most controversial decisions about any development soon would concern traffic flow and parking. The railroad's impact on the town slowly diminished until it disappeared altogether.

The most controversial event of 1937, however, had nothing to do with automobiles. It started innocently enough in July when the Gardenia Packing Company asked the Sausalito City Council for permission to moor the ship *Brookdale* in Richardson's Bay. The *Brookdale* was a floating fish reduction plant used in the production of fish oil. Several years earlier the city had considered a proposal to establish a fish cannery in Sausalito, similar to those on Monterey's "Cannery Row." The plan was rejected because of fears raised about odors emanating from the canning process. But the *Brookdale* was allowed to begin operations after a thousand-dollar bond was posted with assurances that no objectionable odors would be forthcoming. Sausalito residents awoke one morning to the pungent aroma of dead fish. Within weeks the stench had become unbearable. The City Council ordered the *Brookdale* to up anchor and be gone. But the leaky,

old, wooden-hulled vessel had sunk fast in the bay mud and could not be moved. After six months of cajoling, complaining, and threatening, the Gardenia Packing Company refloated the poor old *Brookdale* and towed her away. Early in 1938 the City Council outlawed fish reduction plants in Sausalito, vowing "No more *Brookdale* Affairs."

That action was part of Sausalito's new zoning ordinance, adopted in 1938 after six years of planning and deliberation. For the first time a zoning ordinance acknowledged that Sausalito was first and foremost a residential city, with pockets of commercial and industrial activity, rather than the potential industrial or commercial center some developers had envisioned.

Rumblings of war in Europe became a topic of concern for Sausalitans in the late 1930s. The U.S. Navy once more considered Richardson's Bay as a seaplane base, and there was increased activity at the forts. Fort Cronkhite, established in 1937, was strengthened with additional coastal batteries including fifteen-inch mortars, and security was tightened at military installations all around San Francisco Bay.

As war clouds gathered, Sausalito went about business as usual. Two landmarks vanished in 1940 as the process of change on the waterfront continued. Ray Ellis photographed the sagging old Sausalito Land & Ferry Company office at Bridgeway and Princess Streets in November, 1939 (above). Next to it was Gus Peterson's Pioneer Boat House, a structure dating back as far as anyone could remember. The photo below, taken by Ellis February 24, 1941, shows the same scene after the opening of the new Purity Store.

When England was suffering through the Blitz in 1940, the many Sausalito residents of British descent organized a British War Relief Shop with Edith Wood in charge. Her husband, British-born artist Leonard Sutton Wood, lent his talents to the effort in the form of posters soliciting contributions for "Bundles for Britain" and white elephants for the shop. With U.S. entry in the war, the name was changed to the Allied Relief Salvage Shop, and by late 1943 it was raising over $400 a month for the Sausalito War Chest. After two temporary locations, the volunteers secured a permanent spot on Princess Street in a wood-frame cottage. Today as the Sausalito Salvage Shop, the Princess Street storefront is an ongoing rummage sale, helping to support numerous local charities and the Foster Parents Plan, Incorporated.

*A rare photograph, c. 1939, taken on the eve of World War II. Despite a ban on cameras at the Marin fortifications, a few photographs escaped the censors. This was taken at the instant a fifteen-inch mortar was being test fired. Because of the concussion, the only thing in focus is the gun itself.*

*On February 28, 1941, the* Eureka *made the last regular run to Sausalito for the Northwestern Pacific. Shown here about a week before ferry service ended, the* Eureka *became part of the National Maritime Museum exhibit of historic vessels in San Francisco.*

*Northwestern Pacific Interlocking Tower Number One stands at the Sausalito terminal, c. 1941. It and the tracks remained in place until after World War II.*

*Passengers boarding the few trains left at the Sausalito terminal in late February, 1941. The electric current for the commuter trains was shut off at 3 a.m., March 1, 1941. Regular steam train service lasted until November of that year. Sausalito was a freight "spur track" on the Northwestern Pacific Railroad until 1971.*

*A Northwestern Pacific commuter train speeds southbound into Sausalito after just passing Waldo Point in the late 1930s. It is difficult to imagine the upheaval that will soon transform this quiet tidewater into Marinship.*

*North Sausalito in 1936. The Waldo Grade approach to the Golden Gate Bridge is under construction although the bridge towers in the distance are complete. The future site of Marinship is still a tidal marsh between the new highway through Sausalito and the Northwestern Pacific tracks leading from the railroad yard at the foot of Spring Street. Waldo Point in the foreground has already been carved back slightly during highway construction. Several work boats are clustered at the two piers at Waldo Point and one at the foot of Nevada Street in an otherwise empty bay.*

December 7, 1941: a day that marked the end of an age for America, and the beginning of another. Sausalito was a quiet, bayside town in those days. The railroad and ferryboat era was coming to an end, hastened by the completion of the Golden Gate Bridge just four years earlier. Residents still talked about the controversy over the proposed bridge approach through town, and how construction camps and swarms of workers had given the town a new vitality, helping it climb up from the depths of the Great Depression. Little did the townfolk know that Sunday morning as they huddled around radios, listening to grim news from across the Pacific, that Sausalito was about to experience the greatest upheaval in its history.

The sweeping changes that would transform much of Sausalito's shoreline were already under way within three months after Pearl Harbor. Unlike today, when proposed development must undergo careful scrutiny and survive a myriad of agency and commission hearings, defense construction was given a top priority in the early days of World War II. Zoning regulations and public participation were swept away by the national emergency. Change came with a certainty and swiftness that today seems dazzling.

On March 2, 1942, the chairman of the U.S. Maritime Commission sent a telegram to the W. A. Bechtel Company in San Francisco. It said in part:

IT IS NECESSARY IN THE INTERESTS OF THE NATIONAL EMERGENCY THAT THE MAXIMUM NUMBER OF EMERGENCY CARGO VESSELS BE COMPLETED PRIOR TO DECEMBER 31, 1942. THEREFORE, COMMISSION IS REQUESTING THE MEMBERS OF THE SIX COMPANIES, INC. TO SUBMIT A PROPOSAL AS FOLLOWS: PROPOSED SHIPYARD SITE TO BE LOCATED IN ONE OF THE WEST COAST PORTS IN WHICH YOUR ORGANIZATION COULD OPERATE TO THE BEST ADVANTAGE. THE EMERGENCY DEMANDS ALL WITHIN YOUR POWER TO GIVE YOUR COUNTRY SHIPS.

The Bechtel Company, already busily involved with war work and building Liberty Ships as a member of Six Companies, Inc., began an immediate search for an appropriate uncongested site around the bay. Within twenty-four hours Bechtel fired off a telegram to Washington: SAUSALITO! Six days later, on March 9, Bechtel officials met in Washington with the Maritime Commission with a preliminary plant layout and cost estimate. The same day a telephone call back to San Francisco gave the signal to start. It took three more days for the completed contract to catch up to the project team.

*Marinship officials inspect work in progress, 1942. Left to right: William E. Waste, Vice President and General Manager; Admiral Howard L. Vickery, Vice Chairman, U.S. Maritime Commission; Kenneth K. Bechtel, President of Marinship.*

*Ordinary railroad manifest freight service was inadequate to meet Marinship's needs, and in early 1943 special MTX (Military Train Special) trains were used. The first of these carried main motors, condensers, and parts from Schenectady, New York, via Chicago to Sausalito in 151 hours.*

Within two weeks, the property had been legally condemned and Sausalito and Marin residents informed of the plan; and on March 28, less than a month after the first urgent telegram, heavy equipment tore into Pine Point, overlooking the placid mud flats and marshes of Richardson's Bay. Three months after that, on June 27, 1942, the first keel was laid at Marinship.

After removal of some forty homes from Pine Point, the familiar landmark that jutted out from the Sausalito hills was literally cut in half, ground up, and spewed into Richardson's Bay to become land fill for the shipyard.

Almost 26,000 piles were driven deep into the bay mud. The Northwestern Pacific Railroad tracks were rerouted, and 24,430 feet of new track were laid. A storm drain was put in place, many thousands of feet of water pipes installed, and thousands of yards of asphalt and concrete poured. A huge turning basin was scooped out, and a ship channel 300 feet wide and over a mile long was dug in deep water that would allow ocean-going vessels to penetrate the upper reaches of Richardson's Bay for the first time. In all, some 3 million cubic yards of soils were dredged from the bay bottom. The town fathers of the

*Marinship at peak of production in 1944, looking north, with Marin City in the background. In the left foreground is the main warehouse, the largest building in Marin County at the time (122,500 square feet). Eight new tankers are being prepared for service at the two outfitting docks next to the warehouse. Today this facility is the Army Corps of Engineers Bay Model, and the North pier is used by the Engineers in their bay maintenance program.*

*Steel arriving at Marinship was unloaded at the north end of the yard (top), passed through the huge Plate Shop and Sub-Assembly Shop, and stacked for hull assembly in front of the six shipways. Once a hull was launched, it was towed to the outfitting docks for completion and provisioning for testing and war duty.*

BECHTEL

158

1870s who had envisioned and promoted Sausalito as the "Pittsburgh of the West" would have been proud.

The day and night construction of the launching ways, gantry piers, ramps, and docks awed the local citizenry. As new workers arrived by the hundreds, increasing to 20,000 men and women within the first year, the town's merchants could barely handle the flood of new business generated by the yard. Sausalito's city services couldn't begin to cope with the scale of Marinship. The shipyard had become a city within a city, with training schools, a hospital, cafeterias, police and fire departments. It even had its own railroad system and ferry terminal. In addition, an entire new residential town called "Marin City" was constructed in pastoral Leaside Valley north of Sausalito to house workers and their families, who were pouring in from all parts of the United States. Sausalitans worked at the yard, too. And residents converted every attic, basement, and spare room into bedrooms to accommodate roomers. For many residents, it was a boom time; others considered that Marinship was Sausalito's necessary contribution to the war effort. To some, the monumental changes wrought in their small town were a dark portent of things to come.

World War II brought many people to Sausalito for the first time. Of the many thousands who passed through Marinship's gates in those four hectic years of activity, many of course were local, particularly at first. But soon people from the East, South, and Midwest arrived, by train, by car, even on foot. For some it was love at first sight. They would settle permanently in Sausalito after the war, adding still more regional and international fla-vor to its already colorful melange. The hiring records of Marinship testify to the variety who passed through the gates: people, some of them refugees, from all over Europe, Latin America, Australia, and China—people of every race and color; politicians, actors, lawyers, artists, and athletes; the educated and the uneducated, the skilled and unskilled, the trained and the untrained, converged on the hiring hall. Names on the payroll were as colorful and diverse as the people they belonged to: Ng is there, and Papachristopulos; Annie Obedience, as well, and Orange Mary Green, Empress Lovely, Early Pluck Buggs, and Cave Outlaw.

---

In early 1942 when Sausalito's shipyard was under construction, it had no official name, but was referred to as *Marin Shipbuilding Company,* which was a subsidiary of W. A. Bechtel Company. It soon got an official title as the shipyard of *Marin Shipbuilding Division of W. A. Bechtel Company.* That cumbersome title was soon shortened to *Marin-Ship,* which was used interchangeably as the shipyard name and the company name. Bechtel Company's other shipbuilding division in Long Beach, *California Shipbuilding,* became *Cal-Ship.* In common usage each name became one word, *Marinship* and *Calship.* In newspaper headlines *Marinship* was shortened even more to *M'ship.* By the time the shipyard closed in 1945, the name *Marinship* was a permanent place name in Sausalito, along with Gate 5 Road and Marinship Way.

---

*Marin City was originally a hastily built complex of wartime housing for Marinship workers and their families. On the slopes behind Marin City was Gilead, once the home of Colonel Obadiah Livermore. Built in 1881 near the Old County Road, the main house at Gilead was surrounded by a barn and stables and thirty acres of fruit trees. The pride of Livermore's ranch was his spring water system, with deep cisterns that provided 60,000 gallons a day for his household, stables, and citrus trees.*

At first, each new worker was processed at a vacated house on Pine Point while dynamite explosions rocked the hill as excavations on the shipyard continued. George Keeney, Marinship's Employment Manager (later Mayor of Sausalito), first hired assistants, mainly women who would process workers' applications. One of his first employees was Mary Skarzinski, whose job was to interview prospective workers. On her second day she tried to recruit Kenneth Bechtel, President of Marinship Corporation, when he walked in. He said he was willing to go to work but he didn't have a union card.

Interviews were conducted in the kitchen of the little house and in the Mills Building in San Francisco until June, 1942, when a new hiring hall was opened at 200 Caledonia Street in Sausalito. From this location over the next twenty-four months over 75,000 workers were hired.

Working under enormous pressures of time and shortages, Marinship Corporation built a shipyard; then the engineering department set about its threefold task. First was the EC-2 Liberty Ship program. The second and third were the oil tanker program and the ship repair program.

One department in which Marinship excelled was its "idea factory." Management welcomed all ideas that would speed production, improve safety, or save materials. A system of regular meetings to discuss ideas was instituted, and war bonds were awarded for outstanding suggestions. By October, 1943, Marinship led all other war plants in the nation for war bonds awarded. Among other ideas that outlasted World War II was an automatic bell invented by Marinship workers for moving fork lifts. The bell, fashioned from a brake drum, automatically clanged a warning when the vehicle was moving in reverse. The automatic reverse bell is required by California law on all construction vehicles today.

Morale was high at the shipyard as innovations in work procedures became commonplace. One such was brought about by an increasing shortage of manpower. On July 7, 1942, a new welder showed up for work, creating a minor stir in the work force. Dorothy Gimblett, dressed in new welder's leathers, was the first female yard worker, and something of an experiment by Marinship management. She endured the whistles, grumbling, and laughter of her male counterparts to set a pattern of performance and competency that helped shatter the myth that women could not stand up to shipyard work. By November, 1943, over twenty percent of Marinship workers were women serving as painters, teamsters, shipfitters, machinists, and boilermakers—in fact, in every shipyard capacity. Early resentment by the men soon gave way to admiration as women broke out of clerk-typist roles and became skilled technicians and constructors.

*Security Check at Gate 4*
*From spring of 1942 to winter of 1945, more than 75,000 people from all walks of life passed*
*through Marinship's gates. With that many hastily processed workers from every state in the Union and*
*numerous foreign countries, it was feared that security would be a problem. However, only one incident*
*of attempted sabotage occurred during Marinship's active years.*

Boilers for Marinship's oil tankers were fabricated at the Pacific Erecting Company at 6th and Berry Streets in San Francisco. They were trucked across the Golden Gate Bridge and squeezed through the Waldo Tunnel on Highway 101 by driving the trucks squarely down the center to get clearance.

Construction of the tanker Huntington Hills, launched June 11, 1945, set a record for all World War II shipyards of twenty-eight days from keel laying to launching. She was outfitted and delivered five days later, also a record.

Welders on the outfitting docks in August, 1943, included left to right, Mamie Ray Thompson and Ethel Davidson.

*Each Marinship vessel had a "sponsor" for the launching ceremonies. They were selected by lottery from a name pool of all Marinship employees, from Kenneth Bechtel to the most recently hired worker. The first name drawn was that of yard carpenter Edward H. Winkler, whose wife is shown above ready to do the honors.*

*The moment of truth: 3:30 p.m., September 26, 1942. Mrs. Winkler cracks the champagne bottle across the bow of the* William A. Richardson *as a Marinship executive gives the ship a shove. Over 30,000 people watched the first Marinship launching.*

*After launching, the ships were taken to the outfitting docks (lower left). Here a tanker is made ready for duty.*

The Liberty Ships were creatures of wartime necessity. They were slow and clumsy, but could be built quickly, using readily available skills and materials. Liberties were designed and engineered by Gibbs and Cox and by the California Shipbuilding Corporation, then modified to suit each of the shipyards that were building them. Soon after the first keel was laid in Marinship, the shortage of materials, mainly prime-quality structural steel, became apparent. Overtaxed steel mills had not yet caught up with the overwhelming demands of wartime America. Marinship engineers searched out new sources of structural steel; they dismantled obsolete bridges and steel buildings and even scavenged old laundries for usable parts. In the warehouse of the Northwestern Pacific Railroad in the Sausalito yards, a cache of old steel rails was uncovered, and they soon became part of that first Liberty Ship, the *William A. Richardson.*

Marinship switched to production of oil tankers in the fall of 1942, when oil tankers were being sunk faster than new ones were being built. The T-2 tankers called

*The S.S.* William A. Richardson *moments after launching. Minus most of her deck equipment and supplies, she rides high in the water. During her wartime career the* William A. Richardson *steamed 102,000 miles between Europe, the Pacific, the Mediterranean, and the Persian Gulf, carrying over 60,000 tons of war material and thousands of troops and prisoners of war. After the war she was transferred to the United States Lines.*

*Only one Marinship vessel, the Liberty ship* Sebastian Cermeno, *was sunk in action, and one, the* Francis Preston Blair, *was lost in a Pacific typhoon in 1945. On September 2, 1945, eight Marinship tankers including the flagship S.S.* Tamalpais *were present in Tokyo Bay for the Japanese surrender.*

*Looking like the figurehead on a sailing ship, Admiral Chester Nimitz steels himself for a whack across the nose with a bottle of California champagne. Shipyard artist Charles Pearson decorated the bows of Liberty ships and tankers at Marinship prior to launching. When the vessels were outfitted after launching, these works of art were covered with an anonymous coat of battleship gray.*

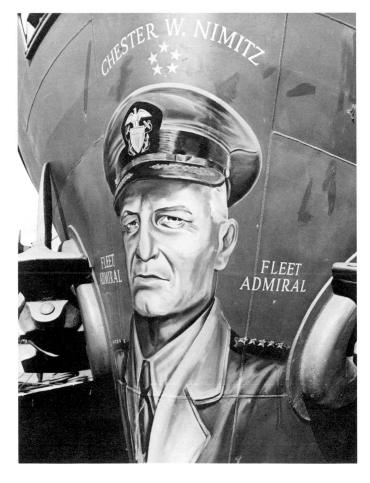

for modifications in shipyard facilities, but soon Marinship hit its stride, launching a new tanker every ten days.

In three and a half years of active service, Marinship produced fifteen EC-2 Liberty Ships, seventy-eight oil tankers, and twenty army invasion barges, outfitted three British coasters, and repaired twenty battle-damaged vessels. Not one Marinship-built vessel ever suffered a major structural or power failure, not even a bulkhead leak.

163

*The tanker* Mission San Francisco *glides into Richardson's Bay from Way Number 6 on September 18, 1945, the ninety-third and last ship launching at Marinship. The event was more festive than most launchings; the Japanese had surrendered a month earlier, on August 15th.*

*The prefabricated barge* Dragon Lady *is launched at* Marinship *in 1945 as employee Frances Jung swings the water jug.*

In the summer of 1945 as the war in the Pacific was drawing to a close, Marinship received a contract to assemble thirty prefabricated steel barges for the army, to be used in Pacific operations. A new site for assembly and launching was developed on the northeast section of the yard so Marinship's main business of tanker construction could continue uninterrupted. Sections of barges were trucked over the Golden Gate Bridge to Marinship to be bolted and riveted together. But an unexpected snag slowed the assembly process. It was nearly impossible to hire skilled riveters since riveting had all but disappeared since the advent of the welded ship. Marinship engineers, always quick with a solution, modified the barges under construction using a combination of welding and riveting. The completed 104-foot-long barges were quickly painted and launched after brief ceremonies. A second order came in for twenty more all-welded barges. But the surrender of Japan in September, 1945, halted all work in progress with nineteen barges completed.

During that same summer, Marinship had been ordered by the Maritime Commission in Washington to undertake a top-secret, vitally important project known only as *Dagwood.* Military planners were proceeding along two avenues of attack to defeat Japan. One was the *Manhattan Project,* the secret development of the atomic bomb. The alternative plan, if the untested bomb failed, was a direct massive invasion of Japan; Dagwood was a key link in the latter program. Each Dagwood was a barge, a floating steel caisson 230 feet long, 70 feet wide, and 60 feet deep, with a blunt bow designed to nest with the concave stern of another Dagwood. Each section, ballasted with concrete and with storage and living compartments below deck, would form part of a breakwater and unloading platform for troops and matériel in the planned invasion of Japan.

Of sixty Dagwoods, plans called for Marinship and Calship to construct twenty-four. The highest presidential priority was issued. Steel mills across the country stopped all other production to roll plates for Dagwood. A twenty-four-hour, seven-day-a-week work schedule was established, and key Marinship workers were assigned to the secret project. Plans were drawn and lines for the barges laid down on the floor of the huge Mold Loft (Industrial Center Building today). Sausalito and the world discovered what the Manhattan Project was on August 6, 1945, when Hiroshima was devastated by the atomic bomb. On August 15, the contract for Dagwood was terminated. The same day, the first two carloads of steel destined for the Dagwood barges arrived at Marinship.

Marinship completed the other vessels under construction at the time of the Japanese surrender. Three more tankers were launched, and by September 25, 1945, the work at Marinship was done. The U.S. Maritime Commission was already in the process of disposing of wartime shipyards. As the unemployed workers scattered to the four winds, the commission suggested to Bechtel Corporation that Bechtel take over the yard, operating it as a government-owned facility, or purchase it for private use. Not eager to get into the peacetime shipbuilding business, Bechtel recommended that the yard become the Army Engineers' operations center for the Pacific Island Reconstruction Program. This idea met with approval all around, and at midnight, May 16, 1946, Marinship became history as the Army Corps of Engineers took over the shipyard.

*Opening Day, beginning of the yachting season, 1945. The parade of boats is seen from* My Toy.
*The large numbers painted on each vessel were part of the security restrictions (including a ban on
cameras in the bay) imposed during World War II.*

With the end of World War II and the closing of Marinship, Sausalitans turned their attention from the waterfront and concentrated on a return to normal, if such a return were possible. Sausalito's population quickly dropped to almost its prewar level of 3,500. The streets and shops seemed deserted when compared to wartime hustle and bustle. As in the rest of the country, shortages of manufactured goods and food rationing still existed, and unemployment was a major cause of concern. The hope that Marinship would continue to provide jobs faded when the Bechtel Company declined to open a peacetime shipyard. The U.S. Army Corps of Engineers needed only a portion of the sprawling facility for their operations, about forty-five acres including the administration building, the warehouse, outfitting docks, and ferry slip. Most of the property was turned over by the U.S. Maritime Commission to the War Assets Administration, whose function was to return government-appropriated property to civilian hands. Marinship was sold off piecemeal by sealed bid auctions. In November, 1946, the first auction disposed

of 181 acres to several new owners. With countless industrial plant closings around the nation, large corporations were simply not interested in the property. Several small businesses did soon open on the site, including the A. G. Schoonmaker Company's diesel engine rebuilding and repair plant. By 1948, thanks to the Northwestern Pacific Railroad's decision to continue service to Marinship rail spurs, business activity had increased. Daily shipments of steel were coming from Cyrus Hasty's salvage company, and King Baldwin's Basic Chemical Company was experimenting with "undisclosed products." The Persolite Company was processing and sacking perlite ore from Nevada for use as a sand substitute in plaster.

In 1949 the Sausalito City Council became interested in a choice seventeen-acre parcel of Marinship property just north of what is now Dunphy Park. The Council negotiated with the War Assets Administration for the waterfront property, which would make an ideal recreation area and municipal yacht harbor. The WAA offered the property to Sausalito for $9,900 cash, one-half of the appraised value, with the restriction that it could be used for recreational purposes only. The city countered with an offer of $9,900 in installments providing "no strings were attached to disposal of the land." The WAA claimed no official bid was received from Sausalito and went on with the sale. The accepted high bid according to the *Sausalito News* was $21,681 from A. G. Schoonmaker for expansion of its diesel engine facility.

In early 1951 Marinship began to serve another, more unexpected purpose. A young couple with a small baby, faced with the critical housing shortage of the period, rented what had been the men's locker room on the top floor of building number 3 (near the launching ways). They removed the lockers and scavenged building material from a nearby structure that had deteriorated beyond repair. Their resulting five-room home prompted two other couples to move into building number 2 next door. The *Sausalito News* applauded the resourcefulness of Sausalito's newest residents and praised their delightful view across Richardson's Bay to Belvedere. "Life is carefree and casual on the ways and each family enjoys its home and neighbors, and each enjoys the satisfaction of its ingenuity in having solved the housing problem."

*Fire Chief Matt Perry poses proudly with Sausalito's new ambulance in 1947, paid for by public subscription. Behind him is the firehouse at Johnson and Caldeonia Streets dedicated in 1940.*

*Part of proposed freeway along Sausalito's waterfront, 1946. The "before and after" photographs graphically demonstrate what could have been, and almost was.*

When enthusiasm for the Golden Gate Bridge ran high in the early 1930s, there was an attempt by a group of Sausalito residents to route Highway 101, the main approach to the bridge, through Sausalito. It was seen as the best way to put Sausalito on the map, to bring prosperity and growth to a sleepy little town. But the Bridge District officials would have none of it. The Waldo Grade approach had already been selected as the main route, and Sausalito would have to be content with a secondary lateral to the bridge.

After the bridge opened in 1937, noise from traffic on the approach made many residents grateful that the main highway had not passed through Sausalito. By 1940 it was conceded by traffic planners that the Waldo Grade approach was inadequate to meet present and future needs. Once again the idea of a major Sausalito lateral surfaced. World War II put highway projects on the shelf for the duration although experience with wartime traffic to Marinship made the need for highway expansion more imperative.

In 1946, with bridge traffic again on the increase, the California Division of Highways submitted seven plans for alternate routes through Sausalito. There were three main designs, each with slight variations. The first and least expensive was a route parallel to the existing one along Waldo Grade. The second was a series of huge viaducts and tunnels through the middle of Sausalito, roughly halfway between the waterfront and Highway 101. The third plan called for a water-level freeway that would swoop down from Alexander Avenue in the south and hug the shoreline for the entire length of Sausalito. This was the route most favored by the trucking industry and safety officials.

When the plans, which had been prepared without Sausalito's participation, were made public, Sausalito residents were aghast. The City Council appointed a Lateral subcommittee composed of Harry Brown, J. Herbert Madden, Carl W. Spring, and Carl F. Urbutt.

The committee quickly concluded that all the proposed plans were detrimental to Sausalito. Engineers Carl Spring and Carl Urbutt in conjunction with Sausalito

artists George Ashley and Leonard Sutton Wood had aerial photographs taken from Alexander Avenue to Waldo Point. These were enlarged, and the proposed waterfront route superimposed on them. The resulting "before and after" pictures shocked residents even more. Sausalito's early opposition stymied the proposal, and by 1951 it was assumed that widening of the existing Waldo Grade was the accepted plan.

But the battle was not over yet. A group called the Northern California Freeway Association advocated a water-level approach once again. And once again Sausalitans spoke out in almost unanimous opposition to it. Fortunately for Sausalito, the cost of acquiring the necessary waterfront property had become prohibitive. In September 1953, work began on the Waldo Grade approach. Ironically, Sausalito had come full circle from the 1850s when no scheme seemed too grandiose to contemplate, when the town had nothing to lose, to the 1950s when the town had a great deal to lose. That same attitude persists today, with residents ready to do battle when they perceive a threat to Sausalito.

*Hulks burning in Richardson's Bay, seen from the* Pacific Queen, *later restored under her original name,*
Balclutha. *During the late 1940s and early 1950s some of the old sailing ships in Richardson's Bay*
*were converted into living quarters and work spaces by artists and writers. Some of the beached vessels met a*
*different fate. On the night of November 17, 1944, the old schooners* Wellesley *and* Santa Barbara *and the*
*freighter* Mazama *were burned near the Madden and Lewis Yacht Harbor, to clear the sand spit of hulks.*
*Hundreds watched as the mayor, with fire chief and city attorney present, ignited an oil-soaked rope leading*
*to the ships. To everyone's surprise, one of the vessels contained thousands of gallons of fuel oil, which*
*burned fiercely through the night. Cities around the bay watched in horror as they assumed Marinship or all*
*of Sausalito was being consumed by flames. The next day as the fire continued, Sausalito was criticized*
*in the San Francisco press for neglecting to inform others of the bonfire.*

$S$ausalito in 1950 was a peaceful small town once again. After the turmoil and the wartime crowds, a quiet settled over the town that had not been experienced in decades. The ferryboats were gone. Steam whistles, for over eighty years a familiar sound to Sausalitans, could no longer be heard. Long lines of automobiles, their occupants impatient to embark for San Francisco, were a thing of the past.  In 1950 weeds grew in the vacant lot where once the Northwestern Pacific depot stood. The ferry slips were slowly rotting away.

The Golden Gate Ferry landing at Princess Street was also abandoned and quiet. The tiny building that once housed Lange's Launch Service had become the Tin Angel, a restaurant and bar. The San Francisco Yacht Club was gone. The imposing clubhouse with its graceful arches was now a bait and tackle shop for local fishermen.

The railroad yards and shops were gone from Sausalito. Many trainmen still lived in town, but there was little activity on the remaining tracks. The locomotives built

in the Sausalito shops were only memories. Old number 20 of the North Pacific Coast Railroad, built in 1900; the novel cab-foreward Number 21, called "The Freak"; the unloved "Electra" built in 1903, all were gone.

The business community of Sausalito in 1950 was still centered around Princess Street and Bridgeway. The shoe repair shop, the Purity Store, Central Pharmacy, the Gate Theatre and Eureka Market, and other small shops were patronized by locals in the days before tourism became an industry. The bars  like the Four Winds and the Plaza were small neighborly places where the bartenders knew everyone who came in. On Caledonia Street, with its own movie theatre since 1943, the pattern was much the same. The Marinship hiring hall had become an auto repair shop once again. Sausalitans still had hopes that Marinship might yet be converted to an industrial plant of one sort or another. Several companies expressed interest in the large marine ways, but the piecemeal dismantling of the shipyard was well under way by 1950.

In the Cove, the old Walhalla was reopened on March 24, 1950, as the Valhalla. Former bordello madam Marsha Owen, better known as Sally Stanford, had purchased the rundown saloon and renovated it in the style of the 1890s. Opening night was like a movie premiere, with music, lights, and notables from San Francisco and a few Sausalito "celebrities" as well.

Richardson's Bay, referred to as the "Boneyard" during the 1880s because of numerous sailing ships laid up there, still had remnants of a windjammer fleet in 1950. Most of them would sail no more. The showboat *Pacific Queen,* ex-*Balclutha* had been towed to Southern California after a brief attempt in 1946 to convert her to a floating poker palace. The *Echo* and *Commerce* were burned before World War II, but the once lovely brig *Galilee* was still there, on the mud near the foot of Napa Street. The steam schooner *Lassen* was beached off the foot of Johnson Street near the rotting bones of smaller vessels.

The waterfront north of Marinship became the final resting place for veteran ferryboats, once worked prodigiously, now abandoned. Here the *City of San Rafael, Vallejo, Charles Van Damme, Issaquah,* and *City of Seattle* eventually were left to their fates. Ironically, these ferry-boats had never been part of Sausalito's past, but served other Bay Area cities. Nevertheless, Sausalito is where they would live out their final chapter, in Sausalito's future. The huge vessels became living quarters and work spaces for artists and craftsmen and in the 1960s became the nucleus around which the houseboat community grew.

Sausalito in 1950 was on the threshold of its "art colony" years. Always a haven for writers, artists, poets, and creative souls of many bents, Sausalito experienced an influx of artists in the decade after World War II. At first some returning servicemen and women may have come to place themselves as far as possible from the insanity and horror of war. They sought the quiet backwaters, as Sausalito was in those days, where natural beauty and serenity abounded. Local artists raised in Sausalito or who came in the 1920s or 1930s welcomed the creative energies released in Sausalito during the 1950s. Art shows held in various places around town over the years evolved into an annual art festival, with established older artists intermingled with newcomers. Many well-known Bay Area artists emerged from the Sausalito art colony of the 1950s. The art festival has become a continuing tradition providing a showcase for local talent.

*Sausalito artists Loyola and Ed Fourtané aboard their home and studio, the old lumber schooner* Lassen, *beached at the foot of Johnson Street, c. 1950. Only the rotted bow of this vessel exists today at the entrance to Pelican Harbor.*

*Princess Street and Water Street, 1910*

*The Bower today is surrounded by trees.*

*Sausalito has managed to retain a human scale.*

*Princess Street and Bridgeway, 1983*

*Bridgeway and Richardson Street today.*

*Sausalito waterfront, 1954*

Sausalito's Historic District, certified in 1980 after years of diligent effort and widespread public support, is shown as it appeared in 1954. The district extends from the old San Francisco Yacht Club building on the left, along Bridgeway north to Mason's Garage, today the Village Fair on the extreme right. It also includes the Casa Madrona Hotel, above Mason's Garage, Laneside, and the commercial buildings along both sides of Princess Street, center in the above photograph.

Any proposed exterior alteration to the structures within the district must be submitted to the Sausalito Historical Landmarks Board and approved by the Community Appearances Advisory Board. Over the years (and before the district was formed), several commercial buildings within the district were "modernized" with glass and aluminum facades, or "antiquated" with pseudo-Victorian gingerbread. But for the most part the historic structures have miraculously survived intact.

*Three of the Wosser ladies, Richardson's Bay, 1908.*

$B$y the late 1940s Sausalito had the form and content that it has today. The elements comprising Sausalito's character were in place: the imprint of early settlers, their yachts and villas, the milieu for diverse skills and crafts. Also present by that time were the impacts of the railroad, highways and ferryboats, Marinship, and innumerable small events that have shaped Sausalito. Events since then have played against this historical backdrop. Changes that have occurred since 1950, for better or worse, have added new facets to Sausalito's character, and these will no doubt become grist for a future historian's mill.

Sausalito's earliest residents would be able to recognize their town today. Unlike many small California towns, Sausalito has retained most of its original contours and many of its first-generation buildings. The value of that lies not so much in preserving the past as in adding content to the present. Sausalito has retained a human scale along with its buildings. Sausalito is not a town living in its past, nor is it oblivious to change. Controversy, a way of life in Sausalito, continues today over development, traffic and tourism, and as usual, politics. The civic concern that stirs controversy also insures that Sausalito will continue to defend itself against those who in promoting the present would destroy the future and lose the past.

Sausalito has been home to many diverse cultures and traditions, from the practical to the flamboyant. But its heritage is that of a cohesive, functioning small town. Through continuing efforts of residents, Sausalito will not lose that heritage.

*Courtney Nievergelt in the Sausalito home of her*
*great-great-great grandfather, Thomas Wosser.*

CHRISTIANSEN

## ANITA KOENIG MEMORIAL PARK

Anita Koenig Memorial Park consists of a small sitting area with a bench at Harrison and Santa Rosa Avenues. This site was dedicated in 1972 to Anita Koenig, a fifty-year resident of Sausalito who gave her time to many civic affairs including the Library Board, The Sausalito Nursery School, the Sister-City Program, tree conservation, and many other activities.

## CAZNEAU PLAYGROUND

Cazneau Playground, a small shady glen just west of Girard on Cazneau Avenue, occupies a portion of the property on which Senator James H. Gardner built his home, the Bower, in 1869, now the oldest residence in Sausalito. In 1962, owner William Matson Roth leased the present playground area to the City for one dollar per month; ten years later he deeded it to Sausalito for "playground and recreation."

## CLOUDVIEW PARK

Cloudview Park is on a triangular portion of the Sausalito subdivision known as Sausalito Heights in 1889. Located at 55 Cloudview Road, this neighborhood playground is landscaped and terraced with a small cottage for community and Recreation Department use. William Matson Roth leased this land to the City in 1962 for one dollar a month; the City received it from him as a gift in 1963.

## CYPRESS RIDGE

Cypress Ridge was acquired in 1976 following a bond issue election for Sausalito's largest open space area— 14.9 acres. Located north and east of Hwy. 101, Cypress Ridge commands a sweeping view of Wolfback Ridge, Mt. Tamalpais, Richardson's Bay, the Tiburon Peninsula, the East Bay, and Angel Island. Over 145 species of plant life can be found in this area.

## DUNPHY PARK

Dunphy Park occupies land and water that was the proposed site of a high-density apartment development. The property was acquired in 1970 for the City with a $560,000 bond issue. A large staff of volunteers did the actual work of turning it into an inviting, tree-filled park with grassy knolls. In 1972 it was dedicated to former mayor Earl F. Dunphy in acknowledgment of forty years of dedicated service to the community. In 1976 the Victorian gazebo was erected, commemorating the United States Bicentennial with a granite plaque. Located between Litho and Bee Streets, east of Bridgeway, this park with its beach is the site of Sausalito's traditional July 4th celebration.

## GABRIELSON PARK

Gabrielson Park is the inviting little grassy area east of the City parking lot with a fine view of San Francisco and the bay. It is on filled land known as the "sandspit," the site of the former Shell Beach. A plaque commemorates the 1968 dedication of the park to Carl W. Gabrielson, "City Councilman, civic leader and internationally known Rotarian." A large metal sculpture in the park is the work of Chilean artist Sergio Castillo.

## GOLDEN GATE NATIONAL RECREATION AREA

Sausalito borders on one of the largest parks of them all. A great portion of Richardson's original *Rancho del Sausalito* has been preserved for public use and enjoyment by its inclusion in the Golden Gate National Recreation Area, created in 1972. Coastal lands including San Francisco's Ocean Beach and Aquatic Park and Angel Island are combined with the Marin headlands and the Point Reyes National Seashore to make over 100,000 acres of open space. It is said to be the largest park adjoining a major metropolitan center in the world. The Secretary of the Interior is charged with preserving the "recreation area, as far as possible, in its natural setting, and protecting it from development and uses which would destroy the natural beauty and scenic character of the area."

## HARRISON PLAYGROUND

Harrison Playground, on Harrison Avenue opposite St. Mary, Star of the Sea Church, was purchased by the City in 1962. This playground occupies a portion of the terraced Victorian gardens of the W. H. Tillinghast house, built in 1872. In true English style the garden was filled with roses, ferns, magnolias, fruit trees, and other specimen trees and flowers. Much of the original garden remains today.

## LANGENDORF PLAYGROUND

Langendorf Playground, on Easterby Street at Woodward Avenue, was a gift to the City in 1964 from Stanley F. Langendorf. Mr. Langendorf used to dock his boat in Sausalito, and when he noticed that the children here played in the streets, he acquired property, had it landscaped, equipped it as a playground, and donated it to the City. The playground was dedicated in 1967.

## MARINSHIP PARK

In 1976, Marinship Park was deeded to the City by the United States Department of the Interior for park and recreational purposes. Located just north of the Army Corps of Engineers Building housing the San Francisco Bay Model, this sunny park area was once covered with machine shops between the big ship ways and outfitting docks of Marinship. Here ninety-three Liberty ships and tankers were built between 1942 and 1945.

## MUNICIPAL FISHING PIER

The Municipal Fishing Pier, also known as Petterson's Pier, to the south of Ondine-Horizons, is the site of the first firehouse, built in 1914 and moved across the street in 1933, where it remains today.

## O'CONNELL SEAT

Sausalito by 1902 felt enough community spirit and municipal maturity to honor one of its own. Poet Daniel O'Connell, who died in 1899, was a Sausalito legend by then, well liked and widely known for his robust independent ways and his lyrical verses. He came to Sausalito in the 1870s and stayed the rest of his life, his creativity flourishing in the slightly Bohemian atmosphere of the town. He lived in a small, brown-shingle cottage with his wife and children in Wildwood Glen, which came to be known as O'Connell's Glen. An early member of the Bohemian Club (1872), O'Connell was associated with the literati of his time: Bret Harte, Ina Coolbrith, Joaquin Miller, and Samuel Clemens.

After his death, close friends and admirers contributed $1,500 to construct this oval stone bench at Bulkley and Harrison Avenues on the spot where O'Connell spent many reflective hours before a panorama of San Francisco Bay. The inscription is from O'Connell's *Chamber of Sleep,* written just ten days before his death.

## PLAZA VIÑA DEL MAR

Plaza Viña Del Mar, constructed in 1904, after North Shore Railroad had filled the land east of Water Street, this small triangular park was granted to Sausalito on the condition that it "be maintained . . . as a public garden or grass plot." What started out as a forlorn little plot of sunbaked grass variously known as Depot Park, Thomas' Park, and Elephant Park became the lush Plaza Viña Del Mar, renamed in 1971 in honor of Sausalito's sister-city in Chile. Located at Bridgeway, El Portal, and Park Street, this park forms the very heart of the Historic District.

## SHELTER COVE

Shelter Cove was acquired as open space in 1960 when a proposed apartment complex and marina would have filled the cove with buildings. In cooperation with the newly formed Sausalito Foundation, the City purchased the underwater lots for open space. The tidelands beyond these lots and all along the city front to Marinship were granted to the City by the State of California.

## SOUTH VIEW PARK

South View Park, on North Street between Third and Fourth Streets, is a three-level playground/tennis court/view-park overlooking the Shelter Cove and San Francisco Bay. South School stood on this site from 1905 to 1958, but it was no longer in use as a school after 1941. The building served as a soldiers' recreation center during World War II and was leased to the City for recreational purposes before being demolished.

## THE SEA WALL

From 1922 to 1937 the Sea Wall just south of Yee Tock Chee Park was a bustling ferryboat landing for the Golden Gate and Southern Pacific Golden Gate auto ferries. During World War II a portion of the platform was fenced off and used by the Navy as a depot for submarine nets. When the land was deeded to the City in 1968, it was specified that the site be used as an "open vista." The Sea Wall continues along the water's edge to Shelter Cove interrupted only by two historic buildings. Twenty-five-foot lots were acquired by the City over the years as they became available mostly in the 1940s and '50s.

## TIFFANY PARK

The pocket-sized Tiffany Park at the foot of the North Street Stairs honors William Zobel Tiffany who served as Sausalito City Clerk from 1913 to 1939. In 1942 when this park was first planned, it was to have been a beach on the east side of Bridgeway. The plans were never completed, and it was not until 1963 that the park was dedicated — on the *west* side of Bridgeway.

## YEE TOCK CHEE PARK

Yee Tock Chee Park was dedicated in 1977 to a much-loved Sausalito merchant, "Willie Yee," proprietor of the Marin Fruit Company. Created from the old Purity Store parking lot and what remained of Princess Park (dedicated in 1961) after Bridgeway was widened, this waterside viewing area is the site of Sausalito's original ferry landing. The ferryboat *Princess* docked here in 1868.

## VALLEY STREET BEACH

Valley Street Beach lies at the foot of Valley Street and along the "underwater" streets Front and Water (Bridgeway). "Old Town" was first mapped in 1851, the underwater streets more clearly delineated in 1871. In 1893, with the town's incorporation, all streets became city property. This has been a favorite walking and picnic beach for many generations of Sausalitans.

---

## NEIGHBORING FORTS

FORT BAKER: Named in 1897 in honor of Col. Edward Dickinson Baker, Commander of the 71st Penns. Infantry Regiment during the Civil War. Killed at the Battle of Balls Bluff, Virginia, 1861.

FORT BARRY: Named Dec. 27, 1904, in honor of Brig. General William Farquhar Barry, commanding 2d Artillery during the Civil War. Participated in capture of Atlanta. Died in 1879.

FORT CRONKHITE: Named in 1937 in honor of Major General Adelbert Cronkhite, commander of 80th Division during WWI.

## MAYORS OF SAUSALITO

Sausalito's mayors are chosen for a two-year term by a simple majority vote by the five-member City Council. The member chosen chairs meetings and serves at official functions. His or her vote remains the same as other members of the Council and does not carry with it a veto power or executive privilege. Prior to 1927 when the governing body was called the Board of Trustees, the mayor was officially called the President of the Board.

| | | | | | |
|---|---|---|---|---|---|
| James W. Sperry | 1893 | Webb H. Mahaffy | 1930 | Philip Ehrlich | 1960 |
| John H. Dickinson | 1894 | J.B. Lowe | 1935 | Paul Micou | 1962 |
| Adolph Sylva | 1900 | J. Herbert Madden | 1936 | Jan Paul Dyk | 1964 |
| Jacques Thomas | 1902 | Fred D. Linsley | 1938 | Melvin S. Wax | 1966 |
| Fred D. Linsley | 1910 | Webb H. Mahaffy | 1942 | Earl F. Dunphy | 1968 |
| Edward V. Baraty | 1912 | John B. Ehlen | 1944 | Alexander R. Imlay | 1970 |
| Charles M. Gunn | 1914 | Clyde Hildreth | 1946 | Robin S. Sweeny | 1972 |
| Charles H. Becker | 1916 | George E. Keeney | 1949 | Evert Heynneman | 1974 |
| E.G. Coughlin | 1917 | Robert Gunn | 1950 | Sally Stanford | 1976 |
| William H. Hannon | 1920 | Sylvester J. McAtee | 1952 | Rene De Bruyn | 1978 |
| J. Herbert Madden | 1924 | Alan H. Scurfield | 1954 | Francis Warren | 1980 |
| Webb H. Mahaffy | 1926 | Robert Goshen | 1956 | Carol Singer Peltz | 1982 |
| Charles Phelps | 1926 | Howard Sievers | 1958 | | |

## MINISTERS OF FIRST PRESBYTERIAN CHURCH, SAUSALITO.

| | |
|---|---|
| Charles G. Paterson | 1902-1907 |
| Elvert Leon Jones | 1907-1909 |
| Arthur F. Feuhling | 1909-1910 |
| W.M. Sutherland | 1911-1915 |
| O.D. Ironmonger | 1915-1917 |
| A.G. Seigle | 1917-1919 |
| John Murdock | 1919-1921 |
| J.E. Burkhast | 1921-1922 |
| W. Stephenson Irvine, S.S. | 1922-1925 |
| R.C. La Porte, S.S. | 1925-1926 |
| J.J. Canoles | 1925-1928 |
| B. Johnson Reemtsma, D.D. | 1928-1935 |
| Alfred Bryce Sidebotham | 1936-1943 |
| Robert Earl Stone, S.S. | 1943-1944 |
| M. Burton Alvis | 1944-1950 |
| Aaron Garnet Miller | 1950-1960 |
| David C. Jacobsen | 1960-1974 |
| George Lincoln McLaird | 1976- |

## SAUSALITO FIRE CHIEFS

| | |
|---|---|
| Arthur Jewett (Fire Marshal) | 1904-1911 |
| W.R. Walker (Fire Marshal) | 1911-1922 |
| W.A. Cook | 1922-1924 |
| Charles Loriano | 1924-1944 |
| M. J. Perry | 1944-1965 |
| C.E. Masten | 1965-1972 |
| Robert Halon | 1972 |
| Robert Quayle | 1972-1976 |
| Stephen Bogel | 1976- |

## SAUSALITO POLICE CHIEFS

From the 1850s to 1893, the year of Sausalito's incorporation, law enforcement for the township was through Justices of the Peace and their constables. After 1875, the North Pacific Coast Railroad maintained their own agents as did the Wells Fargo Express Company. Early marshalls and constables were elected and at times constituted the entire police force.

| | |
|---|---|
| Richard Garrity (Marshal) | 1893-1895 |
| J.E. Creed (Constable) | 1894-1895 |
| J.E. Creed (Marshal) | 1895-1898 |
| John A. Hannon (Marshal) | 1899-1924 |
| Albert F. O'Conner (First Chief) | 1925-1927 |
| James P. McGowan | 1927-1930 |
| Manuel Menotti | 1930-1937 |
| Antone Quadros | 1937-1938 |
| James Doyle | 1938 |
| Antone Quadros | 1939-1942 |
| Thomas Hoertkorn | 1942 |
| James Doyle | 1942-1953 |
| Albert Ingalls | 1953-1954 |
| Louis P. Mountanos | 1954-1958 |
| Howard Goerndt | 1959-1963 |
| Kenneth Huck | 1964-1965 |
| Edward Kreins | 1966-1969 |
| James D. Wright | 1969-1981 |
| William D. Fraass | 1981- |

## PASTORS OF SAINT MARY, STAR OF THE SEA CHURCH, SAUSALITO

| | |
|---|---|
| Patrick Cummins | 1881-1882 |
| Alexander E. de Campos | 1882 |
| P.J. Foley | 1882-1883 |
| Patrick W. Brennan | 1881-1885 |
| John Valentini | 1885-1915 |
| William J. Butler | 1915-1917 |
| Charles R. Baschab | 1918-1939 |
| Michael H. Crotty | 1939-1940 |
| Henry F. O'Flynn | 1940-1965 |
| James M. Moher | 1965-1968 |
| William McGuire | 1968-1971 |
| John Shanahan | 1971-1983 |
| Eugene Duggan | 1983- |

## RECTORS OF CHRIST CHURCH, SAUSALITO

| | |
|---|---|
| Frederick Wilcox Reed | 1882-1889 |
| William Nixon | 1889-1891 |
| Charles D. Miel | 1891-1896 |
| William H. Hamilton | 1897-1900 |
| Andrew C. Wilson | 1901-1904 |
| George Maxwell | 1904-1914 |
| Ross Turman | 1914-1915 |
| Harold St. George Buttrum | 1915-1943 |
| Lloyd A. Cox | 1943-1950 |
| J. Keith Hammond | 1951-1953 |
| Joseph S. Doron | 1953-1964 |
| John Stuart Thornton | 1964-1969 |
| J. Barton Sarjeant | 1969-1978 |
| Robert L. Shearer | 1978-1979 |
| David Robison Breuer | 1979- |

## ORIGINAL PARTNERS OF THE SAUSALITO LAND & FERRY COMPANY

On April 22, 1868 Samuel Throckmorton, John Turney and James Boyd sold 1,164 acres of the Rancho Sausalito to nineteen businessmen for $440,000. They were:

| | |
|---|---|
| Joseph P. Thompson | Charles M. Hitchcock |
| Charles H. Harrison | Frederick A. Bee |
| Anthony Easterby | Joseph de la Montagnie |
| Leonce Girard | John Currey |
| D. William Douhitt | H. B. Platt |
| Edward Bosqui | John L. Romer |
| Maurice Dore | Emile Grisa |
| Henry A. Cobb | J. Clem Uhler |
| Frederick McCrellish | Thomas N. Cazneau |
| William A. Woodward | |

On September 27, 1869, nine of these partners signed articles of incorporation as the Sausalito Land & Ferry Company. They were:

Charles H. Harrison
Leonce Girard
Joseph de la Montagnie
Maurice Dore
Joseph P. Thompson
H. B. Platt
John L. Romer
Henry A. Cobb
John Currey

---

## SAUSALITO, OR SAUCELITO?

The name *Sausalito* has been spelled many ways. Even today when the town is known around the world, the correct spelling apparently is not. Residents receive mail with some curious renditions of Sausalito. The "old" spelling *Saucelito* was actually in vogue from about 1850 until the mid-1880s. Examination of maps and documents, however, indicates that *Sausalito* was actually the original spelling, although some maps have interesting variations on it. A common error occurred when the name was handwritten in script and later translated in type by someone unfamiliar with the town. A handwritten *u* can easily be taken for an *n*, thus *Sausalito* becomes *Sansalito*. As recently as 1881 in an official document naming a new postmaster, the town is identified as *Sancelito*. No doubt to a Washington bureaucrat at the time, if a town was close to San Francisco, it must be called "San"something.

The earliest recorded spelling of the name is the original Spanish designation for the cove: *saucito*, meaning "little willow." It appears in this form on the map accompanying William A. Richardson's 1826 petition for a land grant. Also, in the petition itself, Richardson, who was fluent in Spanish, described the land he requested as being bounded by the *Punta de Bonetas* (corrupted later to Point Bonita), *Playa de Caballos* (Fort Baker), *Saucito, Corte de Madera,* and *Punta de Baulenas* (Bolinas). As noted on the map, *saucito* was not so much a place name as a useful description, and was not even capitalized. The shoreline then consisted mainly of brackish marsh covered with salt water grasses. The cove with its flat beach and willow thickets indicated fresh water seepage. The map notation could just as well have been *agua dulce* (fresh water), but at least *saucito* told mariners what to look for on the shore.

By the 1830s the cove came to be called *Sausalito*. *Sausal,* which translates more accurately as a "willow grove or thicket," was a fairly common appellation in California. Oakland has a "Sausal Creek." Near Los Angeles was the *Rancho Sausal Redondo* or "Round Willow Grove." When Richardson was granted his land in 1838, the deed describes it as *El terreno conocido con el nombre de Sausalito,* "the land known by the name of Sausalito." It was the custom for grantees of Mexican land to name their own ranchos, and they usually settled on something with a nice ring to it, something memorable, or something already well known. Richardson named his grant *El Rancho del Sausalito,* which is certainly more lyrical than the literal "little willow" or *Saucito.*

Throughout his life in his letters in both Spanish and English, Richardson consistently spelled the name of his rancho "Sausalito," never "Saucelito." With the influx of Americans during the gold rush, it became common practice to spell the name *Saucelito,* which is grammatically incorrect in Spanish, a notion that seldom bothered the newly arrived *Americanos.* After California statehood in 1850, *Saucelito* became the accepted spelling on maps and official documents. When Richardson sought to prove his title to the land before the U.S. Land Claims Commission in 1851, he signed his dictated statement in which the clerk had ironically spelled the name *Saucelito.* By that time Richardson was tired and discouraged and no doubt saw the corruption of the name of his *El Rancho del Sausalito* as just one more indignity brought about by the Americans.

The *Sausalito* spelling never completely died out but coexisted with *Saucelito* for the next twenty-odd years. It slowly became the preferred version once again, and in 1887 the U.S. Postal Service officially designated *Sausalito* as the correct spelling, settling the issue once and for all, except for a few diehards.

---

# ORIGINS OF SAUSALITO STREET NAMES

The earliest streets in Sausalito were surveyed by Navy Lieutenant George F. Emmons in 1851 at the request of Charles Tyler Botts, owner of a property purchased from William A. Richardson in 1849. Emmons's map shows a sixteen-block portion of Old Town bounded by South, West, and North Streets, and on the waterfront by Front Street. In all probability Charles Botts assigned names to the streets within these boundaries. Street names included on the original 1851 survey are followed by a single asterisk. (*)

A second map dated March, 1869, shows the streets laid out by the Sausalito Land & Ferry Company by surveyor L. H. Shortt in what became known as New Town. All street names included on this map are followed by two asterisks. (**)

When Sausalito was incorporated in 1893, all streets on both maps plus those added since 1869 were officially accepted. Since incorporation, streets have been periodically added as new areas were developed, and in a few instances, names have been dropped or changed.

When waterfront towns were laid out in the nineteenth century, it was common practice to extend city limits far into bay waters and to show streets on official maps reaching to these limits. In 1868 the California Legislature, under pressure from land developers, gave control of San Francisco Bay tide lands to adjacent cities. In 1870 the California Board of Tide Land Commissioners was authorized to auction off "certain salt marsh and tide lands" to the highest bidder. Underwater streets were given names and deeded by the state to cities. Just as San Francisco had been extended into the bay by filling behind sea walls, it was taken for granted that one day Sausalito's underwater streets would lead to prime real estate. Many of these submerged streets, some of them beachfronts, still exist as legal, city-owned rights of way,

and from time to time figure prominently in waterfront development proposals.

Sausalito also has a network of pathways, usually narrow flights of steps rising from Bridgeway between private homes or buildings. These too are city-owned, public rights of way. Some Marin County cities that once had pathway systems abandoned them when the automobile made hill access easier. But Sausalito's pathways are intact and in their totality a public asset to be treasured.

A few Sausalito street names have either unknown origins or conflicting documentation. It is not recorded who named the streets for the Sausalito Land & Ferry Company, but one can easily imagine an early meeting of the partners when the names of Harrison, Bulkley, Bee, Turney, and Woodward were bestowed upon Sausalito. After that the names got more obscure and more random: Coso and Testa, Litho and Marie. The most intriguing of all was Waldo Street, sandwiched between Sonoma and Myrtle Streets (neither still in existence). The street was never developed, but the name carried over to become Waldo Point and Waldo Station in the railroad era. The street was probably named for William Waldo, a California pioneer and unsuccessful candidate for governor in 1854. Waldo had gold mining interests on the California-Oregon border near "Sailor's Diggings," a rough mining camp. In 1853 when he was campaigning for governor, a town there was named for him. Naturally, all the residents voted for the Whig candidate, William Waldo. It turned out that the town was actually in Oregon, but they kept the name anyway. Several of the Sausalito Land & Ferry Company partners had mining backgrounds and were familiar with small gold camps all over the West. One of them must have suggested the name, either out of nostalgia for early days in the town of Waldo, or to honor an old friend, William Waldo.

---

| | |
|---|---|
| Alexander Avenue | Origin not certain |
| Alta Avenue ** | High road, leading to dairies west of town and to Sunnyhills Cemetery |
| Anchor Street | "A" Street until 1954 |
| Anchorage Drive | (private), leading to Anchorage Apts. |
| Arana Circle | Henry Arana, developer of property |
| Atwood Avenue | Melville Atwood, resident of Sausalito and assayer who confirmed silver content of the Comstock Lode. Prior to 1901, Belknap Avenue, real estate developer. |
| Bay Street | "B" Street until 1954 |
| Bee Street ** | Frederick A. Bee, original partner, SL&FCo. |
| Bonita Street | Pretty (Spanish) |
| Booker Avenue | William Lane Booker, partner in Sausalito Heights development. |
| Bridgeway | Originally Water Street, renamed in 1935. |
| Buchannan Drive | and Court. Origin not certain. Acquired from Sausalito School District in 1963. |
| Bulkley Avenue ** | Col. Charles S. Bulkley, surveyor for SL&FCo. |
| Cable Roadway | Origin not certain. Surveyed in 1889 as possible site for cable tramway. |
| Caledonia Street ** | Third annual Caledonian Games held on this street in 1868. Street realigned in 1936. |
| Canto-Gal | (private) Crowing Rooster (Provincial French). |
| Cazneau Avenue ** | Gen. Thomas N. Cazneau, original partner SL&FCo. |
| Central Avenue | Thoroughfare between Old Town and New Town. |
| Channel Street | "C" Street until 1954 |
| Channing Way | George Channing, Sausalito resident, 1967 |

| | |
|---|---|
| Cloudview Road | Prior to 1937 Cobb Avenue, named for Henry A. Cobb, original partner, SL&FCo. |
| Cloudview Trail | Named in 1937 when it was western edge of Sausalito's corporate limits. |
| Cooper Lane | Dr. C.E. and Minnie Cooper, residents of adjacent property. |
| Crescent Avenue | and Lower Crescent, a geographical description. |
| Crescienta Drive | and Lane. Half-moon (Spanish), 1940. |
| Currey Avenue ** | John Currey, original partner, SL&FCo. |
| Cypress Place | (private), Name of tree. |
| Dolphin Street | "D" Street until 1954 |
| Donahue Avenue | Peter Donahue, pioneer railroad man. |
| Dunn Lane | Origin not certain. |
| Easterby Street ** | Anthony G. Easterby, original partner, SL&FCo. |
| Ebbtide Avenue | Renamed from a portion of Sacramento Avenue, 1960 for Ebbtide Apartments. |
| Eden Roc Drive | (private) named for apartment complex. |
| Edwards Avenue | William Edwards, developer of Edwards-Harrison Tract. |
| El Monte Lane | Named for hillside resort and hotel |
| El Portal | Town Gate (Spanish). Site of welcome arch built in 1908 for Great White Fleet's arrival in San Francisco Bay. |
| Ensign Street | "E" Street until 1954 |
| Excelsior Lane | Once called "Limejuice Alley". Named in 1925 for property owner, Excelsior Loan Company. |
| Filbert Avenue | Origin not certain. |
| Fourth Street * | Part of 1851 Old Town grid. |
| Front Street * | Original waterfront street in Old Town. |
| Gate 5 Road | Security Gate Number Five, Marinship during World War II. |
| George Lane | Robert George, secretary for SL&FCo. |
| Girard Avenue ** | Leonce Girard, original partner, SL&FCo. |
| Glen Drive | and Court. Road to Wildwood Glen, popular picnic spot. Originally Lower Santa Rosa and Naiad Road until 1927 |
| Gordon Street | Origin not certain. |
| Harbor Drive | Road to yacht harbor, 1963 |
| Harrison Avenue ** | Charles Henry Harrison, original partner, SL&FCo. |
| Heath Way | Brian and Edith Heath, ceramicists. |
| Hecht Avenue | Victor Hecht, Sausalito resident. From a portion of Prospect Avenue, 1963 |
| Hi Vista | (private) High road above Old Town |
| Humboldt Avenue** | Alexander von Humboldt, scientist and explorer. |
| Johnson Street ** | Origin not certain, probably Andrew Johnson. |
| Josephine Street | Origin not certain. |
| Kendall Court | Daughter of Kenneth Kidwell, president of Eureka Federal Savings. |
| Laurel Lane | Name of tree. |
| Liberty Ship Lane | Site of wartime shipyard. |
| Lincoln Drive | Origin not certain, probably Abraham Lincoln. |
| Litho Street ** | From Greek *lithos*, meaning stone. |
| Locust Street ** | Name of tree. |
| Main Street * | Site of creek bed leading from hillside springs to shoreline of cove in Old Town. |
| Maple Street ** | Name of tree. |
| Marie Street | Origin not certain. |
| Marin Avenue ** | Name of county. |
| Marinship Way | Boundaryline of shipyard, Marinship, 1963. |
| Marion Avenue | Daughter of J.W. Harrison, developer of Harrison-Edwards Tract. |
| Miller Avenue | and Lane. Orson C. Miller, president of Sausalito Bay Land Company, 1925 |
| Mono Street ** | One (Greek), one block street. |
| Monte Mar Drive | An invented Spanish sounding name for housing tract, 1940. |
| Napa Street ** | Name of county. |
| Nevada Street ** | Name of county. |
| Noble Lane | H.H. Noble, property owner, developer of Sausalito Heights with William Booker. |
| North Street * | Northern boundary of Old Town. |
| Oak Lane | Name of tree. |
| Olima Street ** | Name of town. |
| Olive Street ** | Name of tree. |
| Park Street | Next to *Plaza Vina del Mar* |
| Pearl Street | Origin not certain. |
| Pine Street ** | Name of tree. |
| Platt Avenue ** | Henry B. Platt, original partner, SL&FCo. |
| Princess Street ** | Named for first ferryboat of SL&FCo. |
| Prospect Avenue | Origin not certain. Probably refers to view. |
| Railroad Avenue ** | Underwater street planned as limit of fill area with a seawall similar to San Francisco's Embarcadero. |
| Reade Lane | Purchased from attorney W.F. Reade in 1904. |
| Richardson Street * | Named for William A. Richardson. |
| Ridge Road | (private), top of Wolfback Ridge. |
| Rodeo Avenue ** | Led over ridge to dairy farms in 1869. Trail probably used in Richardson's time for driving cattle. |
| Rose Bowl | (private), named by Erway and Heurkauf families, builders of floats for Rose Parade in Pasadena. |
| Rose Court | Origin not certain. |

| | |
|---|---|
| Ross Road | (private), origin not certain. |
| Saghalie Lane | Straight between Japan and Russia, c. 1905. |
| San Carlos Avenue ** | First Spanish vessel in San Francisco Bay, 1775. |
| Santa Rosa Avenue** | Rose of Lima, first female saint in New World. |
| Sausalito Boulevard | Intended as link between Old Town and New Town with panoramic views. |
| Scenic Lane | Origin not certain, refers to view. |
| Second Street * | Part of 1851 Old Town grid. |
| Spencer Avenue ** | H.K. Spencer, associated with SL&FCo. |
| Spring Street ** | Springs at head of street. |
| South Street * | Part of 1851 Old Town grid. |
| Stanford Way | Sally Stanford, former mayor. |
| Sunshine Avenue | Catches the morning sun. |
| Sweetbriar Lane | Name of home of Captain J.C. Cantwell, Revenue Cutter Service. |
| Testa Street | Spanish for front or forepart. Near edge of 1869 town limit. |
| Third Street * | Part of 1851 Old Town grid. |
| Tillinghast Lane | W.H. Tillinghast, associated with SL&FCo. |
| Tomales Street ** | Name of town and bay. |
| Toyon Lane | and Court. Name of tree. |
| Turney Street ** | John Turney, property owner. |
| Valley Street * | Geographical description, part of 1851 Old Town grid. |
| Varda Landing Road | Jean Varda, artist. |
| Vista Clara Drive | Spanish for clear view. |
| Water Street * | At waters edge on 1851 Old Town map. |
| West Street * | Part of 1851 Old Town grid. |
| Williams Court | Origin not certain. |
| Willow Lane | (private), name of tree. |
| Wolfback Ridge Road | Named by architect Mario Corbett, 1958. |
| Woodward Avenue ** | William A. Woodward, original partner, SL&FCo. |
| Wray Avenue | and Lane. Alban E. Wray, secretary, SL&FCo. |

On May 23, 1868, the main street of Turney Valley was the scene of the third annual Caledonian Games, sponsored by the Caledonian Club of San Francisco. No doubt one or more of the Sausalito Land & Ferry Company partners, perhaps even John Turney, were members of the club. They persuaded the club officers to select Sausalito for the games, which would give the town much needed publicity. The games, attended by over 4,000 people, were reported in a London newspaper: "A fine brass band discoursed music in the spacious pavillion where dancing was kept up the most part of the day; but the great attraction was on the *haugh,* or level green on the bay shore (Caledonia Street), where the games and sports were carried on till the programme was gone through. Verily the image of Scotland lives with her children wherever they go."

Sausalito, in '68, Scene of Caledonian Games

---

THE SAUSALITO HISTORICAL SOCIETY, founded in 1975, is an all volunteer, member-supported organization dedicated to preserving the history of Sausalito.

STAFF December, 1983
Jack Tracy, *Director*
Elizabeth Robinson, *Archivist*
Ann Lyn Sutter, *Editor*
Carol Goforth, *Curatorial Assistant*

BOARD OF DIRECTORS
Vera Clouette
Margaret Rossman
Philip Frank
Evert Heynneman
Marjorie Burke
Fritz Warren

*Research Assistants:*
Neil Shaver
Dave Hodgson
Tom Hoover
*Consultants:*
Rick Bronson, *Legal*
Janet Gardner, *Research*
Glenn Christiansen, *Photo Conservation*
Walt Van Voorhees, *Photo Conservation*
Ted Christensen, *Art Acquisitions*
Jane Breeze, *Paper Conservation*
Harry Goodman, *Video*
Dave Benoit, *Underwater Salvage*

# INDEX

*"The supreme tribute that
one can pay to a city's charms—
is a headlong, lifelong affair."*